A Treasury of Victorious Women's Humor

by
James E. Myers

THE LINCOLN-HERNDON PRESS, INC.
818 South Dirksen Parkway
Springfield, Illinois 62703

A Treasury of Victorious Women's Humor

Published by

The Lincoln-Herndon Press, Inc.
818 South Dirksen Parkway
Springfield, Illinois 62703
(217) 522-2732

Printed in the United States of America

LIBRARY OF CONGRESS CATALOGUING-IN-
PUBLICATION DATA

ISBN 0-942936-35-3 $12.95
Library of Congress Catalogue Card Number 99-095204
First Printing

Typography by

Communication Design
Rochester, Illinois

TABLE OF CONTENTS

INTRODUCTION

As a man who is the editor of 20 collections, books of American Humor with titles all the way from *A Treasury of Husband and Wife Humor* to *A Treasury of Musical Humor*, I have been impressed with the plenitude of jokes extolling the victorious male and the scarcity of jokes extolling the loser — women.

So, I decided to see if I could find enough jokes with the woman the winner and after much searching — for years — I found enough to create this book — a collection of the humor of victorious women.

It took lots of time and research to get the job done. But, at my age, time was no problem and the book you hold in your hand represents the fruit of years of research. So, I hope you enjoy it.

I think you'll agree that a joke book with the woman the constant winner is a unique accomplishment and I, as editor, hope you enjoy reading the book as much as I did assembling it.

CHAPTER ONE

**Laugh and the world laughs with you;
cry — and the world laughs harder.**

How To Figure A Woman

The New Year's dance was in full swing,
Gracefully as puppets on a string,
The pretty ladies ALL arose,
Excusing themselves, "to powder their nose."
Leaving their baffled escorts behind,
Each with this single thought in mind,
"How come women seemed to know,
They'll be able to time it so
That all together they've GOTTA GO."

> Dorothy L. Wampler
> *Motherhood to Menopause*
> 1971

Divorce is God's way of recycling men.

Missing Outhouse

An old lady went out of her house one night to go to the outhouse. She didn't know that they had moved the outhouse that afternoon. When she got to the old place, she fell right into the hole. She was up to her neck in shit. "Fire! Fire! Fire!" she screamed at the top of her lungs.

Pretty soon everybody came running out to where she was. Some of the boys were getting the fire truck ready.

They pulled her out and she was just covered.

"Why did you yell, 'Fire! Fire!'?" they all asked the old woman.

"Do you think anybody would have come if I yelled 'Shit! Shit!'?" she answered.

"Missing Outhouse" is from *Flatlanders and Ridgerunners: Folktales From the Mountains of Northern Pennsylvania,* by James York Glimm, 1983. Reprinted by permission of the University of Pittsburgh Press.

———

Fathers

Bless their hearts, how gallantly,
They lend a helping hand,
Each time a new arrival,
Joins the family clan.
They sweep the floor, burn the trash,
Wash dishes quite intently,
Run all sorts of errands,
Burp the baby gently,
Mind the other children,
Like a regular Pied Piper,
Though rarely do you find one,
Who'll change a stinky diaper.

Dorothy L. Wampler
Motherhood to Menopause
1971

———

Every man has the right to be homely...but he abused the privilege.

———

She looks like a million...every year of it.

"Stick in the Mud, I'd like you to meet Wet Blanket."

Contented

When I gaze upon my image,
Seeing hair of mousy gray,
I think I'll have a dye job,
And wash the years away.
However, as I visualize,
The mess, with all that goo,
Running down my face and neck,
I return and gaze anew.
This time my reflection,
Is not as hard to bear,
I think it rather suits me,
This mousy-looking hair.

> Dorothy L. Wampler
> *Motherhood to Menopause*
> 1971

When husband and wife see eye to eye...they are probably the same height.

Damned If I Will

My only defense for assuming to write,
Is simply, I cannot sleep at night.

My symptom needs no explanation,
It's in the title of this dissertation.

Yet once I started, it became
As though it were some kind of game,

To see how many an application,
Could be applied to MY generation.

The sillier the thought, the duller the chore,
Served to challenge me all the more,

Until I had covered in generality,
The greater extent of my potentiality.

One obvious subject I do know about,
Was one I intentionally left out.

That of my HUSBAND, and I don't guess I should,
Lest our relationship be misunderstood.

I've had a bang-up happy life,
The best part of all is being his wife.

But he's the type of FUNNY GUY,
Who wisecracks at everything I try.

So I swore I'd not lose control,
Any of HIS virtues to extol.

There's no end of merit to his credit,
But damned if I'LL be the one who's said it.

Dorothy L. Wampler
Motherhood to Menopause
1971

—————

Sometimes I wonder if men and women really suit each other. Perhaps we should live next door and just visit now and then.

Katherine Hepburn

8

Love is not the dying moan of a distant violin — it's the triumphant twang of a bedspring.

S.J. Perelman

———————

The woman suddenly lost her husband, and his brother flew in from California for the funeral. The brother had lost his wife only a few months before, and the widow and widower leaned on each other for solace. Soon they fell in love and were married and moved to San Diego.

The woman was bothered by her hasty remarriage so she had a photograph of her former husband framed and put on the piano.

Soon, two of their new neighbors dropped by and asked who the man was in the picture on the piano.

"Oh," said the woman, "that's my brother-in-law. He died about three months ago."

———————

A woman without a man is like a fish without a bicycle.

———————

Greeting Exchange

He goes to work from nine to five,
You spend the day alone.
With a smile you say, "Goodbye."
Smiling, you say, "Hello."

He's off to meetings twice a week,
You spend the evenings alone.
With a smile you say, "Goodbye."
Smiling, you say, "Hello."

He takes a business trip out West,
You spend the week alone.
Tenderly, you smile goodbye,
Warmly, you smile hello.

His company needs a man abroad,
You spend the month alone.
Bravely, you smile goodbye,
With relief, you smile hello.

The clock says it's five-fifteen,
As breathlessly, you dash in,
He shouts his greeting loud and clear,
"Where the Hell've you been?"

Now THAT'S a greeting well worthwhile,
Much more rewarding than if he'd smile.

Dorothy L. Wampler
Motherhood to Menopause
1971

It is better to keep one's mouth shut and be thought a pig than to open it and oink.

Roy Blount, Jr.
What Men Don't Tell Women

A preacher was called to the home of a dying man, not of his congregation. It was very late, but he went and helped the poor guy.

As he went to the door to leave, he said to the man's wife: "I was pleased to come to your sad home tonight, but you aren't a member of my church. Don't you have a minister of your own?"

"Oh yes," the woman replied. "But we couldn't call him out this late at night and expose him to scarlet fever, too."

On Hot Flashes

As GIRLS will do, we chat
About this kind of thing.

Headaches, sleepless nights, and such,
With the trials that they bring.
Though in these discussions,
I have never heard,
Anyone describe a FLASH,
With a clear or concise word.
A Flash," the dictionary says,
"Is a sudden flame,
Over in just a moment."
Webster hadn't played THIS game!
Because, when said flash hits you,
You may be downright sure,
It's not over in a moment,
And they've yet to find a cure.
It starts down at your feet,
Then creeps up to your head,
Like a lobster, freshly boiled,
You lie steaming in your bed.
Or when you're playing bridge,
With some, much younger lasses,
And try to see which card to lead,
Through fogged up, reading glasses.
You may be at a party,
Where you try to figure how,
When everyone is freezing,
You're going to mop your brow.
So when you reach the Flash Age,
And think that's all they'll be,
Remember all I've told you,
And take this tip from me.
Flashes are not Flashes,
That come and quickly go,
They're your private built-in furnace,
That runs an hour or so.

> Dorothy L. Wampler
> *Motherhood to Menopause*
> 1971

The woman walked into a bar and ordered her favorite drink, a martini. She told the bartender to mix it twenty-to-one and the bartender did just that.

The bartender then asked: "Do you want a twist of lemon in it?"

"Certainly not!" the woman shouted. "If I wanted a lemonade, I'd have ordered one!"

GASPIRTZ

**I buried my first husband and cremated my second.
How do you feel about freeze-dried?**

He's such a phony that he gets cavities in his false teeth.

Introduction to Josh Billings

Josh Billings was born in 1818, in Lanesboro, Massachusetts. He was a great humorist who traveled the nation dispensing his humor. Abraham Lincoln said of him, "Josh Billings is the greatest judge of human nature since William Shakespeare."

Here are a few lines from his book, *America's Phunniest Phellow-Josh Billings*. As you see, his spelling was phonetic, very popular in his day and great fun, even today.

Buty

BUTY iz a very handy thing tew hav, espeshily for a woman who aint hansum.

Thare is not mutch ov enny thing more diffikult tew define than buty.

It iz a blessed thing that there ain't no rules for it, for the way it iz now, every man gits a hansum woman for a wife.

Thare iz grate power in female buty; its viktorys reach klear from the Garden ov Eden down to yesterday.

Adam waz the fust man that saw a butiful woman, and was the fust man tew acknowledge it.

But beauty in itself iz but a very short-lived viktory — a mere perspektive to the background.

Thare aint noboddy but a butterfly kan liv on buty, and git phatt.

When buty and good sense jine each other, yu hav got a mixtur that will stand both wet and dry weather.

I hav never seen a woman with good sense but what had buty enuff tew make herself hily agreeable; but I have seen 3 or 4 winmin in mi day who hadn't sense enuff tew make a good deal ov buty the least bit charming.

But, az I sed before, thare ain't no posatiff rule for buty, and I am dredful glad ov it, for every boddy would be after that rule, and sumbody wouldn't git enny rule, besides running a grate risk ov gitting jammed in the rush.

Man buty iz awful weak komplaint — it iz wuss, if possible, than the nosegay disseaze.

If there iz sitch a thing az a butiful man on earth, he haz mi simpathy. Even mithology had but one Adonis, and the only accomplishment he had waz tew blatt like a lamb.

Female Remarks

DEAR Girls, are yu in sarch ov a husband?

This is a pumper, and yu are not required tew say "Yes" out loud, but are expekted tew throw yure eyes down onto the earth, az tho yu was looking for a pin, and reply tew the interrogatory, with a kind ov draud-in sigh, az tho yu waz eating an oyster, juice and all, off from the haff shell.

Not tew press so tender a theme until it bekums a thorn in the flesh, we will presume (tew avoid argument) that yu are on the look-out for sumthing in the male line tew boost yu in the up-hill ov life, and tew keep hiz eye on the britching when yu begin tew go down the other side of the mountain. Let me give yu sum small chunks ov advice how tew spot yure fewter hussband:

1. The man who iz jellous ov every little attenshun which yu git from sum other fellow, yu will find, after yu are married tu him, luvs himself more than he duz yu, and what yu mistook for solissitude, yu will diskover, has changed into indifference. Jellousy isn't a heart-diseaze; it is a liver-komplaint.

2. A mustash is not indispensible; it iz only a little more hair, and iz a good deal like moss and other excressences — often duz the best on sile that won't raize ennything else. Don't forgit that thoze things which yu admire in a phellow before marriage, yu will probably hav tew admire in a hussband after, and a mustash will git tew be very weak diet after a long time.

3. If hussbands could be took on trial, az irish-cooks are, two-thirds ov them would probably be returned; but thare don't seem tew be enny law for this. Therefore, girls, yu will see that after yu git a man, yu hav got tew keep him, even if yu loose on him. Consequently, if yu hav got enny kold vitles in the house, try him on them, once in a while, during courting season, and if he swallers them well, and sez he will take sum more, he is a man who, when blue Monday cums will wash well.

4. Don't marry a pheller who iz alwus a-telling how hiz mother duz things. It iz az hard tew suit these men as it iz tew wean a yung one.

5. If a yung man kan beat yu playing on a pianner, and kant hear a fish-horn playing in the street without turning a back summersett on account ov the musick that iz in him, I say,

skip him; he might answer tew tend babe, but if yu sett him tew hoeing out the garden, yu will find that yu hav got tew do it yureself. A man whoze whole heft lies in musick (and not very hefty at that), ain't no better for a husband than a seedlitz powder; but if he luvs tew listen while yu sing sum gentle ballad, yu will find him mellow, and not soft. But don't marry enny boddy for jist one virtew enny quicker than yu would flop a man for jist one fault.

6. It iz one of the most tuffest things for a female tew be an old maid successfully. A great menny haz tried it, and made a bad job ov it. Evryboddy seems tew look upon old maids jist az they do upon dried harbs — in the garret, handy for sickness — and, therefore, girls, it aint a mistake that yu should be willing tew swop yurself oph, with some true phellow, for a hussband. The swop iz a good one; but don't swop for enny man who iz respektabel jist bekause his father iz. You had better be an old maid for 4 thousand years, and then join the Shakers, than tew buy repentance at this price. No woman ever made this trade who didn't git either a phool, a mean cuss, or a clown for a hussband.

7. In digging down into his subject, I find the digging grows harder the further I git. It iz mutch easier tew inform yu who not tew marry, than who tew, for the reason thare iz more ov them.

   I don't think yu will foller mi advise, if I giv it; and, tharefore, I will keep it; for I look upon advise as I do upon castor ile — a mean dose tew giv, and a mean dose tew take.

   But I must say one thing, girls, or spile. If you kan find a bright-eyed, healthy, and well-ballasted boy, who looks upon poverty az sassy az a child looks upon wealth — who had rather sit down on the curb-stun, in front ov the 5th avenue hotel, and eat a ham sandwitch, than tew go inside, and run in depbt for hiz dinner, and toothpick — one who iz armed with that kind ov pluck, that mistakes a defeat for a victory, mi advise is tew take him boddy and soul — snare him onst, for he iz a stray trout, or a breed very skase in our waters.

   Take him I say, and bild onto him, az hornets bild on to a tree.

On Columbia Discoverin' Woman

Marietta Holley, "Samantha on the Woman Question," 1913

...the figger on the throne wuz so impressive, and the female in front so determined.

Wisdom, and courage, and joyful hope and ardor.

Helped by 'em, borne along by 'em in the face of envy, and detraction, and bigotry, and old custom, the boat sails grandly.

"Ho! up there on the high mast! What news?"

"Light! light ahead!"

But to resoom: a-standin' up on each side of that impressive figger wuz another row of females — mebby they had oars in their hands, showin' that they wuz calculatin' to take hold and row the boat for a spell if it got stuck; and mebby they wuz poles, or sunthin'.

But I don't believe they meant to use 'em on that solitary man that stood in back end of the boat, a-propellin' it — it would have been a shame if they had.

No; I believe that they meant to help at sunthin' or ruther with them long sticks.

They wuz all a-lookin' some distance ahead, all a-seemin' bound to get where they started for.

Besides bein' gorgeous in the extreme, I took it as bein' a compliment to my sect, the way that fountain wuz laid out — ten or a dozen wimmen, and only one or two men. But after I got it all fixed out in my mind what that lofty and impressive figger meant, a bystander a-standin' by explained it all out to me.

He said that the female figger way up above the rest wuz Columbia, beautiful, strong, fearless.

And that it was Fame that stood at the prow with the bugle, and that it wuz Father Time at the hellum, a-guidin' it through the dangers of the centuries.

And the female figgers around Columbia's throne wuz meant for Science, Industry, Commerce, Agriculture, Music, Drama, Paintin', and Literature, all on 'em a-helpin' Columbia along in her grand path-way.

And then I see that what I had hearn wuz true, that Columbia had jest discovered Woman. Yes, the boat wuz headed directly towards Woman, who stood up one hundred feet high in front.

And I see plain that Columbia couldn't help discoverin' her if she wanted to, when she's lifted herself up so, and is showin' plain in 1893 jest how lofty and level-headed, how many-sided and yet how symmetrical she is.

There she stands (Columbia didn't have to take my word for it), there she wuz a-towerin' up one hundred feet, lofty, serene, and sweet-faced, her calm, tender eyes a-lookin' off into the new order of centuries.

And Columbia was a-sailin' right towards her, sterred by Time, the invincible.

I see there wuz a great commotion down in the water, a-snortin', and a-plungin', and a-actin' amongst the lower order of intelligences.

But Columbia's eyes wuz clear, and calm, and deter-mined, and Old Time couldn't be turned round by any prancin' from the powers below.

Woman is discovered.

But to resoom. This immense boat wuz in the centre, jest as it should be; and all before it and around wuz the horses of Neptune, and mer-maids, and fishes, and all the mystery of the sea.

Some of the snortin' and prancin' of the horses of the Ocean, and pullin' at the bits, so's the men couldn't hardly hold 'em, wuz meant, I spoze, to represent how awful tuckerin' it is for humanity to control the forces of Nater.

Wall, of all the sights I ever see, that fountain wuz the upshot and cap sheaf; and how I would have loved to have told Mr. MacMonnies so! It would have been so encouragin' to him, and it would have seemed to have relieved that big debt of gratitude that Jonesville and America owed to him; and how I wish I could make a good cup of tea for him, and brile a hen or a hen turkey! I'd do it with a willin' mind.

I wish he'd come to Jonesville and make a all-day's visit — stay to dinner and supper, and all night if he will, and travel round through Jonesville the next day. I would enjoy it, and so would Josiah. Of course, we couldn't show off in fireworks anything to what he does, havin' nothin' but a lantern and a torchlight left over from Cleveland's campain. No; we shouldn't try to have such doin's. I know when I am outdone.

Bime-by we stood in front of that noble statue of the Republic.

And as I gazed clost at it, and took in all its noble and serene beauty, I had emotions of a bigger size, and more on 'em, than I had had in some time.

Havin' such fellin's as I have for our own native land — discovered by Christopher Columbus, founded by George Washington, rescued, defended, and saved by Lincoln and Grant (and I could preach for hours and hours on each one of these noble male texts, if I had time) —

Bein' so proud of the Republic as I have always been, and so sot on wantin' her to do jest right and soar up above all the other nations of the earth in nobility and goodness — havin' such feelin's for her, and such deep and heartfelt love and pride for my own sect — what wuz my emotions, as I see that statue riz up to the Republic in the form of a woman, when I went up clost and paid particular attention to her!

A female, most sixty-five feet tall! Why, as I looked on
her, my emotions riz me up so, and seemed to expand my
own size so, that I felt as if I, too, towered up so high that I
could lock arms with her, and walk off with her arm in arm,
and look around and enjoy what wuz bein' done there in the
great To-Day for her sect, and mine; and what that sect wuz
a-branchin' out and doin' for herself.

But, good land! it wuz only my emotions that riz me up;
my common sense told me that I couldn't walk locked arms
with her, for she wuz built out in the water, on a stagin' that
lifted her up thirty or forty feet higher.

And her hands wuz stretched out as if to welcome
Columbia, who wuz a-sailin' right towards her. On the right
hand a globe was held; the left arm extended above her
head, holdin' a pole.

I didn't know what that pole wuz for, and I didn't ask; but
she held it some as if she wuz liable to bring it down onto
the globe and gin it a whack. And I didn't wonder.

It is enough to make a stun woman, or a wooden female,
mad, to see how the nation always depicters wimmen in
statutes, and pictures, and things, as if they wuz a-holdin'
the hull world in the palm of their hand, when they hain't, in
reality, willin' to gin 'em the right that a banty hen has to take
care of their own young ones, and protect 'em from the hov-
erin' hawks of intemperance and every evil.

But mebby she didn't have no idee of givin' a whack at
the globe; she wuz a-holdin' it stiddy when I seen her, and
she looked calm, and middlin' serene, and as beautiful, and
lofty, and inspirin' as they make.

She wuz dressed well, and a eagle had come to rest on
her bosom, symbolical, mebby, of how wimmin's heart has,
all through the ages, been the broodin' place and the rest of
eagle man, and her heart warmed by its soft, flutterin' feath-
ers, and pierced by its cruel beak.

The crown wore on top of her noble forehead wuz dretful
appropriate to show what wuz inside of a woman's head; for
it wuz made of electric lights — flashin' lights, and strange,
wrought of that mysterious substance that we don't understand yet.

But we know that it is luminous, fur-reachin' in its rays, and possess almost divine intelligence.

It sheds its pure white light a good ways now, and no knowin' how much further it is a-goin' to flash 'em out — no knowin' what sublime and divine power of intelligence it will yet grow to be, when it is fully understood, and when it has the full, free power to branch out, and do all that is in it to do.

Jest like wimmen's love, and divine ardor, and holy desires for a world's good — jest exactly.

It wuz a good-lookin' head-dress.

Her figger wuz noble, jest as majestic and perfect as the human form can be. And it stood up there jest as the Lord meant wimmen to stand, not lookin' like a hour-glass or a pismire, but a good sensible waist on her, jest as human creeters ort to have.

I don't know what dressmakers would think of her. I dare presoom to say they would look down on her because she didn't taper. And they would probable be disgusted because she didn't wear cossets.

But to me one of the greatest and grandest uses of that noble figger wuz to stand up there a-preachin' to more than a million wimmen daily of the beauty and symmetry of a perfect form, jest as the Lord made it, before it wuz tortured down into deformity and disease by whalebones and cosset strings.

Imagine that stately, noble presence a-scrunchin' herself in to make a taper on herself — or to have her long, graceful, stately draperies cut off into a coat-tail bask — the idee!

Here wuz the beauty and dignity of the human form, onbroken by vanity and folly. And I did hope my misguided sect would take it to heart.

And of all the crowds of wimmen I see a-standin' in front of it admirin' it, I never see any of 'em, even if their own waists did look like pismires, but what liked its looks.

Till one day I did see two tall, spindlin', fashionable-lookin' wimmen a-lookin' at it, and one sez to the other:

"Oh, how sweet she would look in elbow-sleeves and a tight-fittin' polenay!"

"Yes," sez the other; "and a bell skirt ruffled almost to the waist, and a Gainsboro hat, and a parasol."

"And high-heel shoes and seven-button gloves," sez the other.

And I turned my back on them then and there, and don't know what other improvements they did want to add to her — most likely a box of French candy, a card-case, some eyeglasses, a yeller-covered novel, and a pug dog. The idee!

And as I wended on at a pretty good jog after hearin' 'em, I sez to myself —

"Some women are born fools, some achieve foolishness and some have foolishness thrust on 'em, and I guess them two had all three of 'em."

I said to myself loud enough so's Josiah heard me, and he sez in joyful axents —

"I am glad, Samantha, that you have come to your senses at last, and have a realizin' sense of your sect's weaknesses and folly."

And I wuz that wrought up with different emotions that I wuz almost perfectly by the side of myself, and I jest said to him —

"Shet up!"

I wouldn't argy with him. I wuz fearful excited a-contemplatin' the heights of true womanhood and the depths of fashionable folly that a few — a very few — of my sect yet waded round in.

But after I got quite a considerable distance off, I instinctively turned and looked up to the face of that noble creeter, the Republic.

And I see that she didn't care what wuz said about her.

Her face wuz sot towards the free, fresh air of the future — the past wuz behind her. The winds of Heaven wuz fannin' her noble foretop, her eyes wuz lookin' off into the fur depths of space, her lips wuz wreathed with smiles caught from the sun and the dew, and the fire of the golden dawn.

She wuz riz up above the blame or praise — the belittlin', foolish, personal babblin' of contemporary criticism.

Her head wuz lifted towards the stars.

But to resoom, and continue on.

If women didn't exist, all the money in the world would have no meaning.

Aristotle Onassis

She never knew what happiness was until she got married...and then it was too late.

Man

The ways of other creatures seem
Ridiculous in the extreme.

The monk's behavior with his tail
Is something quite beyond the pale.

The camel chews a silly cud;
The hippo bathes in tropic mud.

The serpent never can resist
The tricks of the contortionist.

The whale, for all his glory, blows
Excessive water through his nose.

The idiotic fly will crawl
Along a ceiling or a wall.

But Man, who takes a higher track,
Is merely egomaniac.

> Samuel Hoffenstein
> *Year In, You're Out*
> Reprinted by permission of
> Liverlight Publishing Corporation
> 1930

———————

Perhaps men should think twice before making widowhood
our only path to power.

> Gloria Steinem

———————

Weekends

Saturdays are practical, Sundays are sensual. Actually,
Saturdays as part of the weekend have seriously eroded
since women went off to work and no longer spend their
weekdays picking up the dry cleaning, buying the groceries,
getting the oil changed, calling the plumber, returning the

"He used to catch flies...Now he attracts them!"

library books, taking the dog to the vet and the kids for new shoes, running the vacuum cleaner, mopping the kitchen, scouring the bathtub, recycling the newspapers, addressing the Christmas cards, cleaning the fish tank, and folding the laundry. Now all these matters get pushed ahead, like snow in front of the plow, to bury Saturday, and what was once a day for picnics, sandlot baseball, and pruning roses has degenerated into a day of errands and housework. Nothing good can be said for errands and housework except the twinge of relief at having gotten at least some of them done before nightfall.

Sundays remain. They should be held sacrosanct for idle, luxurious, long-drawn-out sensual experiences, especially sex and breakfast.

Sunday-morning sex is one of the great unsung pleasures. Bedtime sex on weeknights, after a working day, with the flesh wearied and the brain frayed and confused by ordinary matters, the concentration shattered, is all very well, but on Sunday morning, body and soul receptive as a plowed field in May, smoothed and gentled by sleep, unhurried, cradled in leisure, we can stroll through it savoring like a rajah, to the plash of offstage fountains and the harpsong of houris.

Small children who bang on the door should be threatened with death by dismemberment.

Of a Sunday, those who go to church have the added satisfaction of accomplishing their spiritual duty, but some of the idle bloom is rubbed from the day by having to put on stockings or a tie.

The central Sunday meal should take place early, as breakfast or lunch, providing a pivotal point around which the day swings gently. The French understand this principle; their Sunday lunches often last until dark and leave regiments of empty wine bottles and long naps in their wake.

Some find it acceptable at this meal for all hands to read the paper while eating, and I see nothing wrong with this since, compared to its daily version, the Sunday paper is essentially luxurious and frivolous rather than businesslike, and thus less unsociable. By choosing judiciously, it's possible to spend a long and happy day with it and never learn anything ominous. Even the most dignified paper contains splashes of color to mark the occasion; even the sections on world events are less urgent, full of reflective essays on what the past week meant instead of bulletins on today's alarms.

It's a sprawling, generous paper that comes apart into something for everyone, to be traded back and forth across the plates. (One couple I know regularly buys two copies so that each can have a crossword puzzle, but this seems wasteful and a bit unfriendly; the happily shared crossword is a benchmark of the happy marriage.)

Courteous people refrain from reading long excerpts aloud while others are busy with the funnies. Better to give a short exclamation, grunt, or chuckle, and then wait to be urged to share the piece; if nobody urges, don't.

After this central meal, it's customary to find some gentle diversion; in proper weather a spot of golf or a walk in the park, otherwise museums, art galleries, a few turns around the shopping mall or a visit with friends. Nothing essential, nothing practical; respect Sunday. Housework left over from Saturday must be left until next Saturday or perhaps until never. The thorough relishing of leisure is a reliable sign of high civilization and nothing short of appendicitis should interrupt.

The puritanical can tell themselves they're preventing burnout and storing up efficiency for the work-week ahead. The rest of us can simply loll around and tell ourselves it's Sunday.

> Barbara Holland
> *Endangered Pleasures,* by permission of Little, Brown and Company, 1995

Laughter is like the human body wagging its tail.
> *Chinquapin Jones*
> Gravel Switch, Kentucky

"Your toast's ready."

The Ovum

The tiny ovum does not know
Its own capacity for woe.

Oh, nor in bitterness nor in hate
Blame it for its developed state!

It prayed no aching prayer to be
The Son of God, or you or me.

Its hairless hide had little room
For fleas like *cogito* or *sum*.

Lay not to it your daily hurt:
Love came and did the creature dirt.

Who would have thought so small a chalice
Could interest His mighty malice?

It had no thought to injure us
When it beheld homunculus.

It fell, as women often do,
With never a thought of me or you.

And now, alas, it cannot quit
Unless you desensorcel it.

Oh, give the wretched creature gas
And it will gladly go to grass!

Oh, hang yourself and let it be
As innocent again and free!

One slip for love was never meant
To bring such dreadful punishment.

Samuel Hoffenstein
Year In, You're Out
Reprinted by permission of
Liverlight Publishing Corporation
1930

She's awful pretty, but pretty don't make the pot boil.

Mary Isabelle Stewart
Berea, Kentucky

Little Gertrude was visiting her grandmother and among the things they talked about was spanking.

"I bet your daddy doesn't have to spank you very often," Grandma said.

"Not anymore," the little one replied. "Now that I have started to school."

"But how does he discipline you now?" Grandma asked.

"He just talks to me when I misbehave."

"Really! That's all? What does he say?"

"I can't tell you because I never listen."

Wager

You may be an organized wife,
But on this score I'd stake my life.
No matter how handy the closet,
On chair or bedpost he'll deposit
Whatever he's worn the day before.
So it becomes your regular chore,
Before you can make the bed,
To hang up the clothes that he has shed.

Dorothy L. Wampler
Motherhood to Menopause
1971

Rich men are just poor men with money.

"You think that's bad news? I've decided not to get a divorce!"

Proposition No. II

When you're not sure where you're going,
And there are no road signs showing,
Why is it an impossible task,
To get a man to STOP and ASK?

> Dorothy L. Wampler
> *Motherhood to Menopause*
> 1971

A thing worth having is a thing worth cheating for.

> W.C. Fields

"Chew each bite carefully — I can't find my wedding ring."

An Eternal Truth

To celebrate the peace and quiet the day my menfolks were cavorting around the mountain ostensibly in search of the ever elusive elk (I have a sneaking hunch they were doing as much mental unwinding and soaking up high-altitude air and sunshine as hunting), I cleaned the chicken house. Now it doesn't take much mental application to load seven heaping wheelbarrow loads of crud and wheel them to the manure pile to be emptied. I found myself reflecting, as I shoveled, that if there's one thing I've learned in the years since I graduated from the University of Wyoming it is that "A college education doesn't help a bit when you're shoveling manure."

> Phyllis M. Letellier
> *A Stock Tank of Petunias on Poverty Flat* Timber Trails Publishing Co., 1998

———➤●◄———

A man who won't lie to a woman has very little consideration for her feelings.

> Olin Miller

———➤●◄———

Q: How do we know the planet Earth is of the female gender?
A: Because we don't know how old she is.

———➤●◄———

Motherhood Is Fine — if It Weren't for Kids

"Mommy," my three-year-old son asked with a sudden burst of insight, "Have boys drived you nuts?"

Let's face it: If anyone asked me right now (which is unlikely) I'd be inclined to say that motherhood is over-rated. Badly. It isn't that I don't love my children. It is just that they are, well ... children!

As such they have never heard — or at least listened to — all those forgetful grandmotherly types who keep blithely insisting these are the best years of my life. Rather, these relatively normal small boys spend every waking moment (and some sleeping ones) making everything I do at least three times as complicated as it would need to be.

Take a simple action like checking the roast for example. I look back with unadulterated nostalgia on the days when I opened the oven door, pulled the rack out, laid the roaster lid on top of the stove, then went calmly after a fork — if the roast needed turning — or a cup of water — if it needed moisture.

Now checking the roast involves warning the three-year-old that the oven is hot, running down and catching his toddler brother and locking him out of the kitchen, hopefully, with a chair laid down across the doorway, then proceeding with the above activities. Only it doesn't work that way.

About the time I get the oven door open my hyper-active little friend scales the laid-down barrier like it wasn't there and rushes full speed ahead toward the 350-degree oven door. This means I have to intercept him with one hand — which is akin to holding a half-grown bobcat at arm's length — while I check the roast. Then if it needs anything, I put the lid back on, the rack back in and close the door while seeking out fork or water. It also means starting all over to use them.

If I brought the fork and water with me in the first place I (a) probably wouldn't have needed them and (b) the three-year-old would have polished off the water while the toddler glommed onto and then fell on the fork.

Then there is shopping. I used to look forward to my weekly trip to town as a change of pace, an opportunity for some conversation and a gooey, high-calorie treat — a very special part of my week. Now it is a change of pace all right — from a high lope to pell mell. When exposed to the interior of the typical cluttered dime store, that previously mentioned toddler has one speed: hell bent! He crawls out of the stroller faster than I can put him back, unless I tie him in and then he just manages to get frantically tangled in the tethers — protesting at the top of his lungs.

He's too heavy to carry and throws an experienced tantrum when he hits the end of his rope if I try one of those harnesses that seem to work so well on that elite class of society: Other People's Children.

Leaving the kids in the car neither contributes toward their learning to be civilized human beings nor to my peace of mind while shopping. As for something gooey, anything I give them turns into something gooey before they get done with it — as does everything they touch. Shopping is a high point of my week, all right, from which my stamina and morale sink to new lows after each weekly foray.

Another myth involving children and motherhood that borders on being a big fat lie is how they draw Mommy and Daddy so much closer together. If Mommy and Daddy are closer together in this household it is because they are back to back — fighting a losing battle for survival.

I can count on one hand the number of non-child-related conversations we've had in the last three months — and those concerned unpaid bills. The one quiet supper for two we've had since our older son was able to sit in a high chair, both kids were sick in bed with strep throat and we were too worried about them to properly enjoy the peace and quiet. Taking them anywhere with us is pure chaos and leaving them home provides the dual nagging worry of what they are doing to the babysitter and how much each additional minute away from them is costing.

When the doctor said, "He should be way better in the morning," the toddler's 8 a.m., temperature was 104.2 and when that same doctor said (in the emergency room), "Bring him to the office first thing in the morning and we'll get him right in because he's too sick to wait," it took two of us to run him down to take him to the doctor. I keep thinking no one could be as busy as my terrors and not be healthy, but we pay a doctor bill like other people pay rent.

My kids didn't even have the decency to be anything alike. Practically nothing I learned on the first one, a placid timid child, has been applicable to the little bombshell that followed. The hand-me-down clothes don't even fit.

I know I would never have been satisfied until I could join the conversations involving, "What a terrible time I had while I was pregnant with Susie," but sometimes I wonder why I bothered.

Take, for instance, the day I was practically psychotic from answering at least 20 times the same question, asked in the same piercing voice by the same persistent three-year-old, all the while trying to protect my potato salad ingredients — and everything else in the kitchen — from the busy, sticky fingers of his climbing little brother. In a desperate, incoherent move the knife slipped on its way to the onion I thought I was chopping and left a nasty gash in my

33

index finger. I put the knife on a high shelf, wrapped a paper towel around the gushing wound and headed for the bathroom and a roll of bandages I vaguely remembered seeing there some months before.

While the blood-spattered bathroom looked more and more like Custer's Last Stand, I one-handedly moved baby nose drop prescription bottles until I found the bandage box and opening it with my teeth, thinking help was at hand.

I reached in for the roll of gauze and came up with — no kidding — a little fuzzy yellow chenille Easter chick packed lovingly in the gauzeless box by some small boy months before. Heaven only knows where the bandages went! Now I have a new unwritten rule at my house: Look in every container before you put it away.

I suppose with those misguided memories that turn "ye olde swimming hole" into Lake Tahoe and mother's soggy, fallen burnt sugar cake into "the best in the world," I'll some day be guilty of callously telling some frazzled overwrought young mother that she'll look back fondly on the day her baby spilled green food coloring on a pile of freshly ironed tablecloths. If I ever am, I hope she kicks me. Right now, however, I have just one dream.

In it a long yellow wheeled vehicle stops at the driveway with red lights blinking. Two small boys in clean shirts, books in hand, enter the open door of that vehicle. Mommy, watching from the kitchen window, sighs with pure ecstasy as all-engulfing silence descends about her like a silver cloud.

She sits down at the cluttered kitchen table, pours a glass of orange juice and turns her own pages at her own speed while looking over a week-old magazine that still has its cover and all its pages. "I think I'll put a roast in the oven," she thinks, "And make a leisurely shopping trip to town this morning. God bless those dear teachers — I hope their insurance is paid!"

Phyllis M. Letellier
A Stock Tank of Petunias on Poverty Flat
Timber Trails Publishing Co., 1998

How to Lose Friends

I once attended a Golden Wedding celebration. It was enough to make a Mdivani turn over in his grave. Imagine being tied to one man or woman for 50 years! Animals don't do it. Fish don't. Neither does Peggy Hopkins Joyce. Why do humans? An explorer told me recently that elephants, whose life span is frequently 150 or more years, never mate for life. They select a mate when in about their 35th year. The ceremony is very simple. The male elephant slips a sawdust ring over his bride's trunk while the oldest bull elephant of the herd reads aloud from a 1910 copy of the *National Geographic*. This is followed by the pair addressing each other as "Mrs. Helephant" and "Mr. Helephant" and is solemnized by the entire herd's blowing water at them through their trunks. It is called *the Coming of Aitch or Wetting Ceremony*. Thereupon the bride and groom waddle off into the jungle while all the herd trumpets in unison: "May all your troubles be little ones!"

After a week of trying to kid the apes and explorers they meet into believing that they are an old married couple, the pair returns to the herd and is received in an elaborate ceremony in which all the elephants waltz slowly about in a circle like a D.A.R. reception. "Honest, it's a circus!" the explorer told me, and he should know — he's married to the biggest elephant I've ever seen.

Now comes the serious business of married life. The couple sets up housekeeping and all the herd waits around to see if they'll start fighting. Naturally, sooner or later, though it may be ten years or more, a fight starts. If the bride starts the fight she whales the hide off her mate and retires to the bedroom with a loud slamming of the door, taking her mate's hide with her. If the groom starts the fight he does the same to his bride and retires to the furnace room. This is known in the elephant world as *Hide and Go Seek*. In simple English it means if the one who has lost his hide loves the other enough he will go and get his hide back and make up after the quarrel. If he doesn't love the other then he leaves her for good and the couple is considered formally separated.

Isn't that simple? Don't you wish we could be as sensible as elephants? But we can't because our laws forbid it, so we are forced to seek elaborate ways of getting rid of husbands and wives of whom we are tired. What I wish to do is show men and women how they can get divorced if only they are willing to exert themselves a little bit. This chapter is for wives only. For wives who would like a divorce yet can't make their husbands agree to it.

At Breakfast

Be fastidious and regular about appearing in a soiled kimono and curl papers. Don't put a grain of makeup on until after he has left for the office.

See that you slop things on the table and slump into your chair with uncovered yawns and eyes half-opened.

Open his mail. Chatter to him while he attempts to read it.

At Dinner

Never allow your menu to be monotonous. Burn your food one day, undercook it the next.

If he has a favorite dish, serve it to him day after day, and when he objects mildly, whine, "But I thought you *liked* it!"

Place all meat roasts on a too-small platter and see that the carving knife is consistently dull.

Have a centerpiece over which it is impossible to see. Insist on candlelight.

With Other People

Whenever he tells a story interrupt him with, "Darling, I think you've got it mixed up. It was this way — "

Ask everyone if they don't think you are right in certain intimate arguments which you give to them in detail.

Tell all the foolish stories about him you can think of. Incidents like the time he ordered *pate de fois gras* at a restaurant and told you it was from the inside of a cow.

Keep harping on the condition of your furniture and how your husband doesn't earn enough to keep you in stockings.

Regularly interpose: "Don't you think it's time you were getting to bed, dear?"

Make references to his waistline and what he weighed when you first knew him.

Around the House

See that you lose his placemark in books he reads.

Insist upon "cleaning out" and "straightening up" his desk periodically.

Telephone him daily at the office to bring things home from the grocery.

Whenever he wants an opinion from you, reply, "You decide, darling."

Insist upon buying all his neckties for him.

Talk baby-talk and continue to do so when you go out in public with him.

Keep reminding him of all the other chances you had to marry men who are now earning five times what he is getting.

Borrow his razor. Leave stockings in the wash basin. Coat your face with cold cream before climbing into bed.

Keep the light on when he wants to go to sleep so you "can finish a story."

Follow the foregoing suggestions and you'll be mateless quicker than you can say Reno.

So important is the sex side of marriage that I have no right to complete a chapter on "Getting Along Without the Other Person" without recommending a list of books that deal frankly with this problem:

The Unwed Cinema's of Hollywood and Other Maternal Problems by Dr. Will U. Takalook. (Unguarded Press, 2345 Manalive St., Boston, Mass.)

What I Don't Know About Sex! By May Whest. (Hopper Brothers, 456 Madison Street, New York City)

Marital Relations and Other Pests by Wun Long Stae. (I. Merriam, 18 East Contract Avenue, Minneapolis, Minn.)

Sex of One, Half a Dozen of the Other by Doan Tellasole. (Macmillyuns Co., 45 Ninth Avenue, New York City)

Marriage Without Sex and Sex Without Marriage or Which Vice's Versa by Judge Martha

Haightsit. (Blue Ribbon Funk, Inc., 654 Lexington Avenue, New York City)

Sexual Harmony In A. Flat by Dr. Note D. Pallor. (Husband & McBride, Inc., First Place,

Cincinnati, Ohio)

Preparation For Marriage by Dale E. Practice. (Pants Press, Dundee, Ill.)

We all know the saying, "What is home without a mut-ter?" It is up to you as the woman of the house to turn that mutter into a howl for freedom.

Remember:

Many a nightmare has turned into a day nag.

Billie D. Tressler
How to Lose Friends and Alienate People
Reprinted with permission
Stackpole Books, 1937

Money can't buy love but it improves your bargaining position.

———⟫•⟪———

A pretty girl was hired by the supermarket to distribute free samples of a special cheese.

An old friend came by and asked: "I hear you are getting married next month, is that right?"

"Yep! That's correct." "That's great," the friend said, "What are you doing in the meantime?"

The pretty girl replied: "Just giving away free samples."

———⟫•⟪———

"If I were two-faced, would I be wearing this one?"

Abraham Lincoln

"I forgot, is one grunt yes or no?"

CHAPTER TWO

Good taste and humor are a contradiction in terms, like a chaste whore.

— Malcolm Muggeridge

Moonshine

There was a young lady of Rheims,
There was an old poet of Gizeh;
He rhymed on the deepest and sweetest of
   themes,
She scorned all his efforts to please her:
And he sighed, 'Ah, I see,
She and sense won't agree.'
So he scribbled her moonshine, mere
   moonshine, and she,
With jubilant screams, packed her trunk up in
   Rheims,
Cried aloud, 'I am coming, O Bard of my
   dreams!'
And was clasped to his bosom in Gizeh.

Walter De La Mare

—————➤●◄—————

The seven-year-old little girl was going fishing with her father. She left him to go for a walk. Suddenly the father heard a strange cry of pain and hurried after his daughter. Soon he saw a man hopping in agony on one foot. "What happened?" the father asked the guy. "I guess it's my fault, Daddy," the little girl said. "He told me he hadn't had a bite all morning, so I bit him!"

Happiness is having a large, loving, caring, close-knit family in another city.

George Burns

———⊃⊃⊛⊂⊂———

How a Lady Stopped a Train

The Erie Railroad used to run along the Tioga River, sometimes right through a person's backyard. Well, this lady had two pigs killed by the train. So she went up to the depot and told the agent that she wanted the railroad to pay her for the pigs she lost. They refused.

So, the woman went back home and planned her revenge. She had a crock full of grease, and she took it out to the tracks and just spread it all over the tops and sides of the rails for about a hundred yards. Soon the train started coming, and, do you know, the engine's wheels just spun round and round and didn't go nowhere. Men had to get out and wipe off the tracks.

This woman wasn't givin' in yet. She kept greasing the tracks every day for a week. Finally, they just paid her for the pigs.

> "How a Lady Stopped a Train" is from *Flatlanders and Ridgerunners: Folktales From the Mountains of Northern Pennsylvania*, by James York Glimm, 1983. Reprinted by permission of the University of Pittsburgh Press.

———⊃⊃⊛⊂⊂———

A young woman visits a fortune teller. The gypsy peers into the crystal ball and then tells her in a loud voice, "Prepare for tragedy. Your husband is about to die a violent death."

The young woman was quiet for a few seconds, then asked; "Will I be acquitted?"

Grammar Lesson

Sally Dobbius had a hard time learning grammar. So her teacher made her stay after school and write out two hundred times "I have gone, I have gone." When she was finished, she wrote the teacher a note that said, "Dear Teacher, I have written I have gone 100 times and now I have went."

"Grammar Lesson" is from *Flatlanders and Ridgerunners: Folktales From the Mountains of Northern Pennsylvania*, by James York Glimm, 1983. Reprinted by permission of the University of Pittsburgh Press.

———————

Every man wants a woman to appeal to his better side, his nobler instincts and his higher nature — and another woman to help him forget them.

Helen Rowland

———————

There was a girl in Chicago, Illinois whose name was JoAnn Kissinger. She hated the name and had it changed to McVey. A few months later she tired of McVey and had her name changed to Jones. Then, she tired of that name and changed it to Jackson. That didn't suit her, so she changed it to Carter. All of her friends began to ask: "I wonder who's Kissinger now?"

———————

Brother and Sister

'Sister, sister, go to bed,
Go and rest your weary head,'
Thus the prudent brother said.

'Do you want a battered hide
Or scratches to your face applied?'
Thus the sister calm replied.

'Sister! Do not rouse my wrath,
I'd make you into mutton broth
As easily as kill a moth.'

The sister raised her beaming eye,
And looked on him indignantly,
And sternly answered 'Only try!'

Off to the cook he quickly ran,
'Dear cook, pray lend a frying pan
To me, as quickly as you can.'

'And wherefore should I give to you?'
'The reason, cook, is plain to view,
I wish to make an Irish stew.'

'What meat is in that stew to go?'
'My sister'll be the contents.' 'Oh!'
"Will you lend the pan, cook?' 'No!'

MORAL
'Never stew your sister.'

                                 Lewis Carroll

Men who are so dreadfully devoted to their wives are also
apt, from mere habit, to get devoted to other people's wives
as well.

                                 Jane W. Carlyle

Old timer and singer Tony Martin was telling a friend how
difficult life was in Hollywood. "One day," Tony said, "You're
making love with Lana Turner, Betty Grable and some other
cookie, and then the next day you're a has-been!"

"True," said Tony's friend, "But just look and remember
where you has been!"

The guy who boasts that he never made a mistake has a
wife who did.

The woman was having a night out with the girls and time went by so fast that it was morning before she knew it. She was loath to call her husband at home until she hit upon an idea. Then she called and when her husband answered the phone, she said, "Don't pay the ransom money, honey, I escaped."

———>●<———

The girl said to the guy trying to date her: "The next time you pass my house, I'd appreciate it."

———>●<———

So Why Invest in a Man at All?

There are still a number of very sound reasons, and don't listen to anybody who tells you there aren't.

We all have hard practical considerations to take into account. Among them, safety: Living completely alone can be terribly unwise. Self-defense manuals will tell you, "When living alone and answering the door, always yell, 'I'll get it, Bruce!' for the benefit of whatever pervert is lurking on the other side."

Well, I, for one, come from a long line of unconvincing liars. Lying in a low voice is one thing, but lying at extremely high decibel levels is outside the range of many women's capabilities. If a real Bruce will help you sleep nights, and he's making himself available, are you sure you want to fight him off?

Some women insist that pets, and even fine furniture, can fill the same function as men in one's life. Many women swear by cats. Actually, cats are much more difficult than men. Men do not give you small rodents as kiss-and-make-up gifts, men do not try to eat everything smaller than they are, and men do not require tiny little doors just to be let out of the house.

Many women insist that living with a man is a hindrance to getting to know one's "selfhood." But living with one's "selfhood" has become inconvenient for a number of reasons. It is difficult to share the rent with one's selfhood. It is difficult to fold sheets with one's selfhood. It is very silly to bring one's selfhood home to meet one's parents since, pre-sumably, you've already met.

But I won't kid you with a lot of cogent reasoning and fancy talk and intricately crafted arguments —

The Main Reason to Live with a Man:

You will never have to go on dates again. The principal difference between dates and Nazi torture is that Nazi tor-ture took place in the 1940s and was seriously criticized at the Nuremburg trials. Dating, however, is STILL LEGAL and remains one of the least-understood atrocities that humans can commit. (Why, one wonders, is "to date" a transitive verb — something you do to another person? You could replace the verb "to date" with "to offend," "to assault," or "to dive-bomb.")

ANY NORMAL WOMAN OUT OF HIGH SCHOOL WHO DOES NOT WANT TO THROW UP BEFORE A DATE IS PROBABLY ON DRUGS, OR MENTALLY DEFICIENT. (For what it's worth, this is probably true of men, too.)

Casual dating (which is already a contradiction in terms) brings up so many irksome, niggling questions:

- Will you enjoy each other's company?
- Will you laugh at the same places in the movie?
- Will you agree, afterward, that you've *seen* the same movie?
- Will he want to pay for the meal?
- Will you need to pay him for paying for the meal?

If you are living with a man you do not have to worry about whether you should sleep with him after dinner. Which is to say, you'd bleeding well *better* sleep with him; but at least it's a black-and-white issue — there are no fine points of law involved. And if you are living with a man, he won't respect you any less in the morning than he does now.

A lot of women say, "I'm afraid to live with a man. He'll know *everything* about me."

Every woman has an "It" about herself that she doesn't want known. Something private and dark and terrible. Lizzie Borden, for example, had a tough time on evenings out after she was acquitted, whenever her date said, "So, do your folks live in the area?" Once you begin living with a

45

man, though, he forgives many of your trespasses, and you
even forget rapidly what dates used to be like: God is merci-
ful. (All you have to do is spend an evening with a single
friend and *her* date to remember the horror of it all over
again. Watch the anguish on your friend's face as her date

mispronounces "Fassbinder" or makes Chinaman jokes or eats his salad with his oyster fork.)

Another Good Reason

Living with a man means, at least theoretically, not having to sit home and wait for him to call. You will look back with amazement on the days when you were expecting a call from some Special Guy. You canceled all your appointments for two days, filled a Hefty bag with Doritos, and camped out by the phone table. Sometimes you turned the phone upside down to see if all the wires were connected. When the phone rang, it was your mother, and you screamed into the receiver. Then you waited some more.

When darkness fell, you did not turn on the lights. You did not turn on the television or read a book, because your heart was pounding so fast that the excitement of reading *Martin Chuzzlewit* yet again would give you a coronary. You rehearsed the nonchalant tone you would affect when the call finally came.

Only it didn't.

Further Good Reasons

People often decide to live together simply because they need more personal contact in an impersonal world. Some claim this "contact" can be provided just as easily by one's immediate family, or even by another *woman*, but they are mistaken. Living with your family after the age of twenty-one is admitting that they have a Monopoly on your life. It is returning to "GO" without collecting two hundred dollars.

As for female roommates: They are indeed kind, loyal, thrifty, brave, and obedient; as well as modern and politically acceptable to other women. But all too often living with another woman is like waking up in the middle of a Rona Jaffe novel. Do you really want to spend the rest of your adult life arguing about who ate the last Figurine? Can another woman give you grandchildren?

And there can be no better reason for favoring men than this: esthetics. All male roommates at 7 A.M. look appreciably rumpled, yet adorable. They exude innocence, huggableness — a sort of helpless, charming *je ne sais quoi*.

"I want something to relax my husband...
Do you have anything that smells like poker chips?"

All female roommates at 7 A.M. look like Lon Chaney. No one knows why this is true, but it is.

Stephanie Brush
Men: An Owner's Manual
Reprinted with permission of Simon
& Schuster
1984

Marriage is the alliance of two people, one of whom never remembers birthdays, and the other who never forgets them.

Ogden Nash

————≫●≪————

The candidate and his wife got home after a strenuous day of electioneering. They took off their shoes and fell into chairs when the husband admitted, "Wow! I'm exhausted. What a day!"

"I'm the same," his wife replied. "I can't recall ever being this tired."

"You're tired! Why should you be tired? I'm the one who had to make all the speeches."

"I'm tired because I had to listen to all those speeches!"

————≫●≪————

A husband is a guy who thinks twice before saying anything.

————≫●≪————

I have a simple philosophy: fill what's empty, empty what's full, and scratch what itches.

Edith Wharton

————≫●≪————

Following a bad automobile accident that left one person lying in the street, seriously injured, a crowd gathered around the man. Then a woman pushed through the crowd and began to help the injured man. But, quickly she was pushed aside by a man who said, "Sorry to push you, lady, but I've had a course in first aid and can help this fellow."

The lady stood, stepped aside and let the man work on the patient for a brief time, then said, "When you get to the point where you've done all you've learned to do from your fist aid course, and where it tells you to call a doctor, I'm already here."

"George! Supper's ready!"

If only we'd stop trying to be happy, we could have a pretty
good time.

Edith Wharton

There Was an Old Person in Gray

There was an Old Person in Gray,
whose feelings were tinged with dismay;
She purchased two Parrots,

and fed them with Carrots,
Which pleased that Old Person in Gray.

Edward Lear

————>»•«<————

Happiness is not a goal, it is a by-product.

Eleanor Roosevelt

————>»•«<————

The woman waited until her husband was through with supper and seated in front of the TV set. Then she went to her room and changed into a cocktail dress and came out to walk stylishly before him. "Honey, this is my new dress. I think it is just perfect to wear to the cocktail party we're going to next week. How do you like it?"

"Take it back," he said. "It's awful. Ugly. I don't want to be seen with you wearing that terrible dress."

"That's what I hoped you'd say, dear," wifey replied. "This is my old cocktail dress...now I can go buy a new one. Thanks, honey."

————>»•«<————

I never hated a man enough to give his diamonds back.

Zsa Zsa Gabor

————>»•«<————

My grandmother was a very tough woman. She buried three husbands. Two of them were just napping.

Rita Rudner

————>»•«<————

A woman was having a cup of coffee with her neighbor and remarked: "I feel real good today, I gave a bum five dollars...that made me feel wondrously good."

"You gave a bum five dollars? That was a lot of money to give away, especially to a bum. What did your husband have to say about that?"

"Oh, he agreed with me doing it. He said 'thanks'!"

Rich men are just poor men with money.

Actually, it only takes one drink to get me loaded. Trouble is,
I can't remember whether it's the thirteenth or the
fourteenth.

George Burns

"Don't interrupt your father when he's listening to me."

Platonic love is love from the neck up.

Thyra Samter Winslow

A New York woman lived in an apartment with valet parking. One morning she called for her car just two weeks

before Christmas and headed for her job. On the dashboard she noticed a colorful card reading: "Merry Christmas from all the men in the garage."

She didn't give it much thought until just two days before Christmas when she saw another card reading: "Merry Christmas from all the guys in the garage — second notice."

———⟫⟩•⟨⟪———

Two girlfriends over coffee: "Why is it, Maizy, that you have never married?"
Maizy: "Why should I? Who needs it! I have a dog that barks, a parrot that uses four-letter words, and a cat that's gone all hours of the night.

Things Men Say to Women

I never loved another person the way I loved myself.

> Mae West

———>●<———

A woman was called for jury duty and the court attorney was questioning her.

"What is your occupation?" he asked.

"Housewife," she replied.

"And your husband's occupation?"

"He's a manufacturer," she said.

"Children?" she was asked.

"Nope. He manufactures baseballs."

———>●<———

Whenever you want to marry a man, go to lunch with his ex-wife.

> Shelley Winters

———>●<———

Home Management

The man you marry may be perfect,
However,
With a bit of training from you,
He will improve.
Just remember!
Classes should NEVER be held in public.

> Dorothy L. Wampler
> *Motherhood to Menopause*
> 1971

———>●<———

In politics, if you want anything said, ask a man; if you want anything done, ask a woman.

> Margaret Thatcher

Gene Perret's Funny Business:
Speaker's Treasury of Business Humor
For All Occasions

Business Dress For Success (Women)

- Try to wear clothes that are so nice that men will feel compelled to fold them neatly when they undress you with their eyes.
- If male executives think ties are a pain in the neck, you wonder what they'd think of panty hose?
- Panty hose are different from ties. You don't tie a knot in panty hose; they just feel like someone did.
- A power suit for women executives is one that makes you look tough enough to smile despite your panty hose.
- Women in the office should appear attractive but not seductive. Unfortunately, they have to dress for success and self-defense at the same time.

"Well, would you marry me if I wasn't such a low-life little creep?"

- Sexy attire is not proper for the work place. Some women not only look like they were poured into their dresses, but forgot to say when.
- If mini skirts return, some women executives will have to opt for early retirement.
- The male chauvinist pig is still around, but humor won't let him be much more than a ham. As John Wayne used to say, "A woman's place is in the home and she ought to go there just as soon as she gets off work."
- "I've determined it's not God's will for women to wear miniskirts. If it were His will, He would have created flesh-colored varicose veins." — Erma Bombeck
- One spouse said, "My husband just sits around the house in those ratty clothes on the weekend and I'm ashamed of him. If company comes, I paint a black line on top of his bald head and tell them he's a piggy bank."

  "Or I just stick a piece of ivy in his beer can and tell them he's a planter."
- A meat packing firm demanded for health and safety reasons that the workers wear specific uniforms on the job. Many of the women objected because the prescribed dress was neither sexy nor flattering.

  The company had to enforce the dress code strictly, but attempted to keep morale up by offering to buy a new dress for every female employee. They were told to pick out a dress and send the bill to the company.

  They all did, but one employee got somewhat extravagant. She sent a bill to the company for $300. The bill was brought all the way to the company president. Although he agreed the employee was a little greedy, he ordered that the bill should be paid anyway. He said, "I've packed a great number of hogs in my day, but this is the first time I've ever dressed one."

> Gene Peret and Linda Peret
> from *Funny Business: Speaker's Treasury of Business Humor For All Occasions*
> Reprinted with permission of Prentice Hall Direct, 1990

There are two kinds of women: those who want power in the world and those who want power in bed.

Jacqueline Kennedy Onassis

No, we rarely ever have any sexual harassment here..."

Shirley was an alcoholic and one day she met her priest who gave her a strong lecture on the evils of drink. "If you continue drinking as you do," the priest admonished her, "you'll get smaller and smaller and eventually turn into a mouse."

This scared the daylights out of Shirley and she returned home to tell her husband about her experience. She finished by telling her husband; "If you should see me getting smaller and smaller, dear, will you kill that damned cat of ours."

Three senior citizens were talking about their health and other things. "What would be your choice if you were told you only had six months to live?" Going on she said, "I'd cash in all that I own and take a trip around the world."

"I'd do about the same thing," another said. "I'd cash in all my stocks and bonds and spend the money visiting my kids and grandkids, scattered around the country."

They both looked at the third woman and asked, "What would you do?"

"I'd go at once to see another doctor," was the reply.

The woman speaks eighteen languages and can't say "no" in any of them.

> Dorothy Parker

Two women were enjoying a bit of excessive drinking and on the way to their homes, they wandered into a funeral parlor. They staggered about until one fell over the piano.

"Here's the coffin," she said to the other.

"Do you know the guy in it?" asked her friend.

"No, but he sure has a great set of teeth," she replied.

I'm not embarrassed to be with a younger man except when I drop him off at school.

> Angie Dickinson

Marge: "How much would you pay for my husband?"
June:　　"Nothing."
Marge: "OK. You bought him."

The honeymoon is surely over when he phones home to tell her he'll be late for dinner and she's already left a note that it's in the refrigerator.

Four women were playing bridge and talking. One woman said, "My husband just got back from Paris and brought me 24 bottles of perfume, six ounces to each bottle at $50.00 per ounce. The tragedy is that I'm allergic to perfume and can't use the stuff."

"Allergies are truly awful," one woman replied. "My hubby brought me a full-length mink coat , but I can't wear it...I'm allergic to mink."

The third woman spoke up. "It's the same with me. My husband bought me a diamond ring encrusted with pearls, but I can't wear it because I'm allergic to diamonds."

The fourth woman suddenly stood and rushed to the bathroom where she vomited for ten minutes.

When she walked back to the card table, one woman said, "How terrible! What caused you to get sick like that?"

"I guess it's because I'm allergic to horse shit," was the reply.

———➤●◄———

Women and elephants never forget.

Dorothy Parker

———➤●◄———

The wedding night found Pat and Clarissa in a lovely suite with a bottle of champagne by the bed. The bride pulled a sexy nighty out of her traveling bag just as hubby pulled off his pants and threw them at her, telling her to put them on.

The derned pants fell down around her ankles and she said, "Sweetheart, I can't get these on," as she handed them back.

Now you understand!" he shouted. "I'm the man and I wear the pants in this family."

The girl slipped out of her panties and tossed them to her husband telling him, "Put these on sweetheart."

Of course the guy couldn't get them past his knees and said, "I can't get into your pants, dear!"

"That's right!" she snapped back, "And it'll be that way until you have a change of attitude."

"I'm in love with Sean! I want to own him, possess him, devour, enslave and control his every thought and deed! Other than that, not much new... and you?"

Q: Why is beauty more important for a woman than brains?
A: Because plenty of men are stupid, but only a few are blind.

If love is the answer, could you rephrase the question?
                                        Lily Tomlin

Three guys die and go to heaven. St. Peter asks them if they've been faithful to their wives. The first guy admits to two acts of unfaithfulness during his marriage. St. Peter gives him a midsize car to drive in heaven.

Then St. Peter asks the second guy if he'd been faithful to his wife and he replied, admitting to just one affair. St. Peter gives him a compact car to drive in heaven.

St. Peter asked the third man about his faithfulness to his wife and he said he'd never been unfaithful. So, St. Peter gives him a luxury car to drive in heaven.

The men drive off and a few days later they are stopped side by side at a red stoplight. The men in the compact and midsize cars notice the other fellow sobbing away in his luxury car. They ask him what was the matter and that they thought he ought to be laughing with that luxury car to drive.

The guy replies to their inquiry: "I just passed my wife. She was on a skate board.

————⟫●⟪————

Tom was on his death bed with his wife, Polly, by his side. Haltingly, he says, "Polly, I got to tell you..."

Polly put her finger on his lips and said, "don't talk now. Be still."

"No," hubby says, "I must tell you. I want a clean conscience when I get to heaven. I've been unfaithful to you."

Polly replies: "I know. Why do you think I poisoned you?"

————⟫●⟪————

The longer I live, the more beautiful life becomes.

Frank Lloyd Wright

————⟫●⟪————

A lawyer and his wife were having a heavy argument at breakfast. Afterward he said: "I gotta tell you...you ain't so good in bed, either."

By noon, though, he decided to try to patch things up at home, so he called his wife on the phone. Finally, she picks up.

"What took you so long to pick up the phone?" he asks.

"I was in bed," was her reply.

"What the heck were you doing in bed this late in the morning?" he demanded.

"Getting a second opinion," was her reply.

———>≫●≪———

Take an interest in your husband's activities...hire a detective.

———>≫●≪———

An archeologist is the best husband a woman can have; the older she gets, the more interested he is in her.

Agatha Christie

———>≫●≪———

Lucy asked Edith, "What would you do if you found a woman in bed with your husband?"

"With him?" Lucy replied, pausing a moment to think about it... "Let's see now, first I'd break her cane, then I'd shoot her seeing-eye dog, then go to the phone and call a cab to take her back to the institution she came from."

———>≫●≪———

Love is an ocean of emotions surrounded by expenses.

James Dewar

———>≫●≪———

R-e-m-o-r-s-e

The cocktail is a pleasant drink,
It's mild and harmless, I don't think.
When you've had one, you call for two,
And then you don't care what you do.

Last night I hoisted twenty-three
Of these arrangements into me;
My wealth increased, I swelled with pride;
I was pickled, primed and ossified.

R-E-M-O-R-S-E!
Those dry martinis did the work for me;
Last night at twelve I felt immense;
Today I feel like thirty cents.
At four I sought my whirling bed,
At eight I woke with such a head!
It is no time for mirth or laughter —
The cold, gray dawn of the morning after.

If I ever want to sign the pledge,
It's the morning after I've had an edge;
When I've been full of the oil of joy
And fancied I was a sporty boy.
This world was one kaleidoscope
Of purple bliss, transcendent hope.
But now I'm feeling mighty blue —
Three cheers for the WCTU!

R-E-M-O-R-S-E!
The water wagon is the place for me;
I think that somewhere in the game,
I wept and told my maiden name.
My eyes are bleared, my coppers hot;
I try to eat, but I can not;
It is no time for mirth or laughter —
The cold, gray dawn of the morning after.

George Ade
1866-1944

———————

The most popular labor saving device today is still a husband with money.

Joey Adams

63

H.B.

That rather jolly rum-looking man over there,
So kind to all and some, warm and debonair,
As fat as a plum and as soft as a slug —
His Christian name is Hum, and his surname is Bug.

                                          A.B. Ramsay

———————

And Her Mother Came Too

I seem to be the victim of a cruel jest,
It dogs my footsteps with the girl I love the best.
She's just the sweetest thing I have ever known,
But still we never get the chance to be alone.

My car will meet her — And her mother comes too!
It's a two-seater — Still her mother comes too!
At Ciro's when I am free, at dinner, supper or tea,
She loves to shimmy with me — And her mother comes too!

We buy her trousseau — And her mother comes too!
Asked *not* to do so — Still her mother comes too!
She simply can't take a snub, I go and sulk at the club,
Then have a bath and a rub — And her brother comes too!

There may be times when couples need a chaperone,
But mothers ought to learn to leave a chap alone.
I wish they'd have a heart and use their common sense
For three's a crowd, and more, it's treble the expense.

We lunch at Maxim's — And her mother comes too!
How large a snack seems — When her mother comes too!
And when they're visiting me, we finish afternoon tea,
She loves to sit on my knee — And her mother does too!
To golf we started — And her mother came too!
Three bags I carted — When her mother came too!
She fainted just off the tee, my darling whisper'd to me
'Jack, dear, at last we are free!' — But her mother came to!

                                          Dion Titherage
                                          1889-1934

The Perfect Husband

He tells you when you've got on
Too much lipstick
And helps you with your girdle
when your hips stick.

Ogden Nash

"Some men are born great and some have greatness thrust upon them...my Ed sleeps."

Reflection on Babies

A bit of talcum
Is always walcum.

Ogden Nash

The Parent

Children aren't happy with nothing to ignore
And that's what parents were created for.

Ogden Nash

———————

Grandchildren don't make a man feel old; it's the knowledge that he's married to a grandmother.

G. Norman Collie

———————

Fatigue

I'm tired of Love: I'm still more tired of Rhyme
But Money gives me pleasure all the time.

Hilaire Belloc

———————

Q: How long do you have to stay at a party to get credit for going?
A: You have missed the point. Credit is what you get by returning something that you have bought or charged, for instance brandy snifters. In most department stores, the transaction is made by computer and will show up on your next bill.

Unfortunately, this type of business is out of the question in most homes, so you'll have to steal a knickknack, preferably one of great real or sentimental value. A piece of antique jewelry would be nice; a prescription drug will do. Mail whatever you have selected back to your host a few days later, and you'll get the credit you need.

Patricia Marx
Excerpts from *You Can Never Go Wrong By Lying*
Reprinted by permission of Houghton Mifflin Company
Text copyright (c) 1985 by Patricia Marx

Every girl should use what Mother Nature gave her before Father Time takes it away.

Laurence Peters

———⟫●⟪———

A man and his wife were driving down a country road when they were stopped by a sign: "Road Closed — Do Not Enter." In spite of his wife's urging him to turn around, the stubborn guy ignored the sign and drove ahead. A few miles down the road they came to a bridge that was out and he was forced to turn around and retrace his path. His good wife said not a word. She didn't have to. As they approached the sign, the back of it read: "Welcome back, stupid!"

———⟫●⟪———

Not Tonight, Josephine

Though I have an admiration for your charming resignation
(There appears no limitation to your constant animation)
And a deep appreciation of your warm cooperation,
And I find a consolation in the pleasing contemplation
Of a coy anticipation quite beyond articulation,
Yet forgive the implication if I plead disinclination
For the sweet exhilaration of a brief amalgamation.
I'll tell you in a phrase, my sweet, exactly what I mean:
...Not tonight, Josephine.

Colin Curzon

———⟫●⟪———

The only time a woman wishes she were a year older is when she is expecting a baby.

Mary Marsh

———⟫●⟪———

Q: Is it wrong to borrow your friend's brand-new luggage?
A: Your friend has brand-new luggage lying around the house because she uses her old luggage when she travels.

She does not want her new luggage to become shabby, for then she would have two sets of old luggage. That would be senseless. She might as well have not bought the new luggage.

If you borrow your friend's new luggage, your friend's system will be ruined, and she will lose much sleep figuring out how to remedy it. That is no way to treat a friend. You could borrow your friend's shabby luggage, but then you would be embarrassed in the baggage pickup area. What you should do is borrow your friend's unused luggage, and when you return home, buy her a new set. This is a nice way to say thank you and it makes everyone happy.

> Patricia Marx
> Excerpts from *You Can Never Go Wrong By Lying*
> Reprinted by permission of Houghton Mifflin Company
> Text copyright (c) 1985 by Patricia Marx

———⟫●⟪———

To bring up a child the way he should go, travel that way yourself once in a while.

> Josh Billings (1818-1885)

———⟫●⟪———

Inspect Us

Out of the clothes that cover me
    Tight as the skin is on the grape,
I thank whatever gods may be
    For my unconquerable shape.

In the full clutch of bone and steel
    I have not whined nor cried aloud;
Whatever else I may conceal,
    I show my thoughts unshamed and proud.

The forms of other actorines
    I put away into the shade;

All of them flossy near-blondines
　　Find and shall find me unafraid.

It matters not how straight the tape,
　　How cold the weather is, or warm　—
I am the mistress of my shape　—
　　I am the captain of my form.

　　　　　　　　　Edith Daniel

"I should've realized he was immature when he registered us
for our wedding shower at Toys R Us."

It's a good thing that beauty is only skin deep or I'd be rotten
to the core.

　　　　　　　　　Phyllis Diller

Aunt Jean's Marshmallow Fudge Diet

Fred Allen used to talk about a man who was so thin he could be dropped through a piccolo without striking a single note. Well, I'm glad I never met *him*; I'd hate to have to hear about *his* diet.

I can remember when I was a girl — way back in Truman's Administration — and No-Cal was only a gleam in the eye of the Hirsch Bottling Company. In those days it was fun to go to parties. The conversation used to crackle with wit and intelligence because we talked about *ideas* — the aesthetic continuum in Western culture, Gary Cooper in Western movies, the superiority of beer over lotion as a wave-set, and the best way to use left-over veal.

Go to a party now and the couple next to you won't say a word about the rich, chocolate texture of their compost heap or how practical it's been to buy bunk-beds for the twins. They won't talk about anything except their diets — the one they've just come off, the one they're on now, or the one they're going to have to start on Monday if they keep lapping it up like this.

I really blame science for the whole business. Years ago when a man began to notice that if he stood up on the subway he was immediately replaced by *two* people he figured he was getting too fat. So he went to his doctor and the doctor said, "Quit stuffing yourself, Joe." And Joe either stopped or he didn't stop, but at least he kept his big mouth shut. What was there to talk about?

Today, with the science of nutrition advancing so rapidly, there is plenty of food for conversation, if for nothing else. We have the Rockefeller diet, the Mayo diet, high-protein diets, low-protein diets, "blitz" diets which feature cottage cheese and something that tastes like thin sandpaper, and — finally — a liquid diet that duplicates all the rich, nourishing goodness of mother's milk. I have no way of knowing which of these takes off the most weight, but there's no question that as a conversation-stopper the Mother's Milk Diet is way out ahead.

Where do people get all these diets, anyway? Obviously from the magazines; it's impossible to get a diet from a newspaper. For one thing, in a newspaper you can never catch the diet when it *starts*. It's always the fourth day of Ada May's Wonder Diet and, after a brief description of a simple slimming exercise that could be performed by anybody who has had five years' training with the ballet, Ada May gives you the menu for the day. One glass of skim milk, eight prunes, and three lamb's kidneys. This settles the matter for most people, who figure — quite reasonably — that if this is the *fourth* day, heaven deliver them from the first.

However, any stoics in the group who want to know just how far Ada May's sense of whimsy will take her can have the complete diet by sending twenty-five cents in stamps to the newspaper. But who has twenty-five cents in stamps? And if you're going to go out and get the stamps you might as well buy a magazine which will give you not only the same diet (now referred to as *Our Wonder Diet*) but will, in addition, show you a quick and easy way to turn your husband's old socks into gay pot holders.

In a truly democratic magazine that looks at all sides of the picture you will also find a recipe for George Washington's Favorite Spice Cake which will replace any weight you may have haphazardly lost on that wonder diet.

If you have formed the habit of checking on every *new* diet that comes along, you will find that, mercifully, they all blur together, leaving you with only one definite piece of information: French fried potatoes are out. But once in a great while a diet will stick in your mind. I'll never forget one I read about last summer. It urged the dieter to follow his low-calorie meals by performing a series of calisthenics in the bathtub. No, not in the bathroom. I read it twice, and it said in the *bathtub*. What a clever plan! Clearly, after you've broken both your arms you won't be able to eat as much (if at all) and the pounds will just melt away. In fact, if you don't have a cooperative husband who is willing to feed you like a two-year-old you may be limited to what you can consume through a straw, in which case let me suggest that Mother's Milk Formula.

**How many happy marriages do you know about
where the ladies are still wearing size 12?**

The best diet I've heard about lately is the simplest. It
was perfected by the actor Walter Slezak after years of careful experimentation. Under the Slezak plan, you eat as
much as you want of everything you don't like. And if you
should be in a hurry for any reason (let's say you're still
wearing maternity clothes and the baby is eight months old)

then you should confine yourself to food that you just plain hate.

Speaking about hateful food, the experts used to be content with merely making food pallid — by eliminating butter, oil, and salt. Not any more. Nowadays we are taught that, with a little imagination and a judicious use of herbs, anyone can turn out a no-calorie dish that's downright ghastly. Just yesterday I came across a dandy recipe for sprucing up good old boiled celery. You just simmer the chopped celery (with the tops) in a little skim milk. When it's tender, you add chopped onion, anise, chervil, marjoram, a dash of cinnamon, and you have a dish fit for the Dispose-All. And you'd better have a Dispose-All, because it's awfully messy if you have to dump it into a newspaper and carry it out to the garbage can.

And where is all this dieting getting us? No place at all. It's taken all the fun out of conversation and all the joy out of cooking. Furthermore, it leads to acts of irrational violence. A friend of mine keeps all candy and other luscious tidbits in the freezer, on the theory that by the time they thaw out enough to be eaten she will have recovered her will power. But the other night, having been driven berserk by a four-color advertisement for Instant Brownies, she rushed out to the freezer, started to gnaw on a frozen Milky Way, and broke a front tooth.

But let's get to the heart of the matter. All these diets that appear so monotonously in the flossy magazines — who are they for? Are they aimed at men? Certainly not; most men don't read these magazines. Are they intended for fat teen-agers? Probably not; teen-agers can't afford them. Do not ask for whom the bell tolls. It tolls for you — Married Woman, Mother of Three, lumpy, dumpy, and the source of concern to practically every publication in the United States. And why, why is the married woman being hounded into starvation in order to duplicate an ideal figure which is neither practical nor possible for a person her age? I'll tell you why.

First, it is presumed that when you're thinner you live longer. (In any case, when you live on a diet of yogurt and boiled grapefruit, it *seems* longer). Second, it is felt that when you are skin and bones you have so much extra energy that you can climb up and shingle the roof. Third — and this is what they're really getting at — when you're thin you are so tasty and desirable that strange men will pinch you at the A & P and your husband will not only follow you around the kitchen breathing heavily but will stop and smother you with kisses as your try to put the butter back in the icebox. This — and I hope those in the back of the room are listening — is hogwash.

Think of the happy marriages you know about. How many of the ladies are still wearing size twelve? I've been giving this a lot of thought in the last twenty minutes, and I have been examining the marriages in my own troubled circle. What I have discovered is that the women who are being ditched are one and all willowy, wand-like, and slim as a blade. In fact, six of them require extensive padding even to look flat-chested.

That the fourteen divorcees, or about-to-be divorcees, whom I happen to know personally are all thin may be nothing more than a coincidence. Or it may just prove that men don't divorce fat wives because they feel sorry for them. Then again — and this is rather sinister — men may not divorce fat wives because they imagine that the poor, plump dears will never locate *another* husband and they'll be paying alimony to the end of their days. (I mention this possibility, but my heart's not in it.)

The real reason, I believe, that men hang onto their well-endowed spouses is because they're comfy, and nice to have around the house. In a marriage there is nothing that stales so fast as physical beauty — as we readers of *Modern Screen* have observed. What actually holds a husband through thick and thick is a girl who is fun to be with. And any girl who has had nothing to eat since nine o'clock this morning but three hard-boiled eggs will be about as jolly and companionable as an income-tax inspector.

So I say, ladies, find out why women everywhere are switching from old-fashioned diets to the *modern* way: no exercise, no dangerous drugs, no weight loss. (And what do they mean "ugly fat"? It's *you*, isn't it?) For that tired, run-down feeling, try eating three full meals a day with a candy bar after dinner and pizza at eleven o'clock. Don't be intimidated by pictures of Audrey Hepburn. That girl is nothing but skin and bones. Just sit there smiling on that size twenty backside and say, "Guess what we're having for dinner, dear? Your favorite — stuffed breast of veal and corn fritters."

All your friends will say, "Oh, Blanche is a mess, the size of a house, but he's crazy about her, just *crazy* about her!"

> Jean Kerr
> *Please Don't Eat the Daisies*
> Used by permission of Doubleday, a
> division of Random House, Inc.
> Copyright (c) 1957 by Jean Kerr

God, for two people to be able to live together for the rest of their lives is almost unnatural.

> Jane Fonda

Q: What should you do if you're at a funeral and you can't stop laughing?
A: Though it is in excellent form to cry at a wedding, by some bizarre logic, it is considered rude to laugh at a funeral, even if the deceased died the way Mama Cass did, with a ham sandwich in her mouth. The survivors of the deceased are hurt, and therefore, you should try as hard as you can not to laugh. This will make you laugh harder and harder until eventually, tears will stream down your cheeks, and everyone will be happy.

> Patricia Marx
> Excerpts from *You Can Never Go
> Wrong By Lying*
> Reprinted by permission of Houghton
> Mifflin Company
> Text copyright (c) 1985 by Patricia
> Marx

"I guess it was mean — I put sleeping pills in his Viagra bottle."

CHAPTER THREE

A laugh a day keeps the psychiatrist away.

Heredity is what a man believes in until his son begins to act like a delinquent.

The Widow's Protest

One of the saddest things that ever came under my notice (said the banker's clerk) was there in Corning, during the war. Dan Murphy enlisted as a private, and fought very bravely. The boys all liked him, and when a wound by-and-by weakened him down till carrying a musket was too heavy work for him, they clubbed together and fixed him up as a sutler. He made money then, and sent it always to his wife to bank for him. She was a washer and ironer, and knew enough by hard experience to keep money when she got it. She didn't waste a penny. On the contrary, she began to get miserly as her bank account grew. She grieved to part with a cent, poor creature, for twice in her hard-working life she had known what it was to be hungry, cold, friendless, sick, and without a dollar in the world, and she had a haunting dread of suffering so again. Well, at last Dan died; and the boys, in testimony of their esteem and respect for him, telegraphed to Mrs. Murphy to know if she would like to have him embalmed and sent home; when you know the usual custom was to dump a poor devil like him in a shallow hole, and *then* inform his friends what had become of him. Mrs. Murphy jumped to the conclusion that it would only cost three or four dollars to embalm her dead husband, and so she telegraphed "Yes." It was at the "wake" that the bill for embalming arrived and was presented to the widow.

She uttered a wild sad wail that pierced every heart, and said, "Sivinty-foive dollars for stooffin' Dan, blister their sowls! Did thim divils suppose I was goin' to stairt a Museim, that I'd be dalin' in such expinsive curiassities!"

The banker's clerk said there was not a dry eye in the house.

Mark Twain
American Publishing Company
1875

When you consider what chance women have to poison their husbands, it's a wonder there isn't more of it done.

Kim Hubbard

One Perfect Rose

A SINGLE flow'r he sent me, since we met.
    All tenderly his messenger he chose;
Deep-hearted, pure, with scented dew still wet —
    One perfect rose.

I knew the language of the floweret;
    'My fragile leaves,' it said, 'his heart enclose.'
Love long has taken for his amulet
    One perfect rose.

Why is it no one ever sent me yet
    One perfect limousine, do you suppose?
Ah no, it's always just my luck to get
    One perfect rose.

Dorothy Parker
1893-1967

I am a woman meant for a man, but I never met a man who could compete.

Bette Davis
1908-1989

Q: If your financial life is very simple because you make no money and have virtually no assets, should you do your own taxes?

A: You should never do anything you can pay others to do, even if you can't afford it.

> Patricia Marx
> Excerpts from *You Can Never Go Wrong By Lying*
> Reprinted by permission of Houghton Mifflin Publishing Company
> Text copyright (c) 1985 by Patricia Marx

The spiritual superiority of women is a gift from God.

"One day the wife was cleaning house and decided to throw out everything that didn't work."

A High Toned Woman

In a song made popular by Tennessee Ernie Ford, the male in "Sixteen Tons" complains that, among other troubles, "ain't no high toned woman make me walk the line." From one hardworking man's point of view, high toned women should be avoided. Such a woman might want to improve upon or change the naturalness of a man who could load sixteen tons. In contrast, and in words from a modern translation of Old Testament sentiment, a good woman of Jack County was laid to rest with these works, "She is a worthy woman, high toned, more valuable than rubies and her husband and family rise up and call her blessed." Who then was this creature, this High Toned Woman, feared and suspected by some, venerated and adored by others? Did she really exist? And when? Can we take her dimensions, test her worthiness, name her parts, examine her, proclaim her riches? And how does the High Toned Woman fit into the great chain of being and on the ladder of other female types — mothers, others, doormats, schoolmarms, Lesbians, Amazons, and the liberated who can "bring home the bacon, fry it up in the pan, and never ever let you forget you're a man"? Where do we find her, how do we identify her, rescue her, and name a movement after her? Can we actually find one to call by name and to bestow upon her the label *folk heroine*? To answer all these deep, deep questions "which lie too deep for tears," is the purpose of this paper. And in view of the past Sesquicentennial year of 1986, when women were hung on the line naked for all the world to see and were the subject of papers, seminars, university courses, discussion groups, town meetings, banking services, support shelters, counseling sessions, half-way houses, hospital facilities, and even books, it is my purpose to take one long, last look at a type which has, up to now, been completely and thoroughly neglected and, by so doing, to lay completely to rest one more female type on the "sunny slopes of long ago."

Who or what were High Toned Women? They were those women in every small community who counted themselves as the authorities in matters both temporal and spiritual, but mostly spiritual. They could organize, direct, conduct, and orchestrate feminine matters; could fine tune, refine, regulate, and monopolize the female psyche; and could judge, draw, and quarter unworthy opponents. They were looked up to, respected, and emulated for their clear judgment, their unerring fortitude, their dogged pursuit of truth as they saw it, their unflagging dedication to showing the rest of us how to live. They were the nearest thing a community had to folk heroines, and they strutted in a hen yard just big enough to accommodate them.

High Toned Women were found in rural communities where little contact and influence from the outside world was possible, or else there was just enough contact to get matters all mixed up and to pick out the most glaring faults of the civilized city and cast them in country molds. Churches served as the community clubhouses, so to speak, and were the meeting grounds several times a week for not only High Toned Women but every other variety. Opportunities were many to practice the female arts in Sunday School, which in some churches was an all-female group, Sunday morning worship, Training Union, Sunday evening services, Wednesday evening prayer meeting, women's missionary groups, choir practice, weddings, funerals, Bible Study, and class socials.

Although High Toned Women might be viewed anywhere in the community from the post office to the bank to any store around the square, they were on display in all their glory in church. I fellowshipped with the Baptists, but Methodists, Pentecostals, Churches of Christ, and Presbyterians had choice entries in the High Toned category too. They scratched and clucked in their own yards and only rarely got in each other's way, sometimes at a revival. Usually there were no more than three to any given territory. It seemed to be the rule, however, that whatever denomination held a revival, the visiting High Toned Women yielded to the women in the presiding church.

Within the church, High Toned Women were most obvious in the choir, usually in the front row in the soprano section. Sometimes a fine alto got in on the ladder, but altos sat behind the sopranos; therefore the front-row soprano had the upper hand. At times, deep emotion, or perhaps contrition, during the closing hymn played upon the face of a High Toned Woman as the words (or perhaps the sound of her own splendid voice) moved her to shake her head, close her eyes, take out her handkerchief, let her voice break (for a moment only and never long enough to cause her to lose control of her pitch), and gasp for a moment. Did anyone come forward? Ah well, perhaps another verse. High Toned Women paid no attention to the choir director, but rather let the spirit, through them, lead the choir, the preacher, and the entire flock into ten more verses. High Toned Women always know best the mood and disposition of the Holy Spirit. I have often wondered if the custom of the "long call" was instituted by a High Toned soprano and not by any pleading preacher.

Personally, I learned early to take the cue from the choir. The long call was unnecessary. I plunged down the aisle at every opportunity at every revival, every church, and gave my heart to whatever cause was pending — missionary work at the stop sign at the edge of town, praying on the street, singing on the curb, teaching on the sidewalk, persuading by the wayside. Religiously, I've been on more street corners than the *Dallas Times Herald*. It became obvious and alarming to my family that by the time I was twelve, I was a High-Toned-Woman-In-Training — a docent in the museum of rural high society.

It was not in the choir, however, that High Toned Women worked the hardest. It was in the congregation on Sunday mornings and "amongst" the masses at revival. Although there were some variations on the grand theme, almost all High Toned Women were large and fleshy women, wore corsets, had hour-glass figures, donned hats and gloves for all religious occasions, and carried black purses with strap handles. When they came into the aisles from the back of the church or arbor, their entrance reminded of great ships at sea as they turned their bows into the wind. Sailing relentlessly on to the front with their summer-weight dresses rippling and flapping like sails in their own breeze, we felt the platform tremble and the planks of the benches moan as their well-staved masts groaned and creaked against the rigging of their underwear.

It was in the church aisles that the real power of a High Toned Woman was sometimes wielded. When the invincible ironsides turned her guns on sin and sinners who ought to be at the altar, the smoke billowed, the air hung heavy with the smell of fire and brimstone, and it seemed indeed that "the earth did shake and the veil of the temple was rent in twain," as a High Toned Woman wrestled during the long call with the devil in the soul of some misguided youth or hardened husband. And no one could keep his head bowed and his eyes closed *too*, for we all wanted to witness the power of a tongue in flames as the High Toned Woman pleaded, exhorted, and called down God Almighty and a few angels to assist her in bringing a lost soul home. Her voice intoned, "Oh, sinner, if just one soul like you is saved tonight, the angels in heaven weep." That was probably no exaggeration. Meanwhile, in the choir another High Toned Woman jumped into another verse of "Almost Persuaded" to assure her sister of a little more time with the stubborn, hardheaded, nastly little sinful son-of-a-saint.

There may have been High Toned Women in cities. We often speculated that there might be some in Dallas, but we never knew for sure. We knew Fort Worth was a big town, but still a country town and their ways were not the stranger's ways. But Dallas! Dallas was such a dangerous place and we didn't go — hardly ever. All the women there were Quality, which is not the same as High Toned or the same as Choice or Prime. I had Quality explained to me once in Dallas, by my grandmother. Mama Hartman took me once, when I was a small girl, inside the very walls of Neiman-Marcus. We kept to the sides of the store, never venturing into the aisles except to get to another wall. She allowed me to look swiftly at whatever goods were on eye level, but she kept a firm grip on my hand. The ladies who were shopping paid no attention to us, and so I got to look at them all I wanted. What I saw was Quality.

"We are going to hunt the bathroom."

"But, Mama, you told me never to go to the bathroom in a strange house and never, never in a department store 'cause you never knew who'd been usin' the pot. You said, if you were desperate, never to sit on the seat — never — but to hunker above it. And then when you do go, it leaves the seat all wet all over it and you either have to clean up or else not let anybody see you leave because they'd know you were the one who did it on the seat. You said it was better to hold in no matter what; and to always go to the bathroom the last thing before you left the house. Mama, I don't need to use Neiman-Marcus' bathroom." I was pulling back now and whispering so she wouldn't shush me.

"I know all that, Joyce Ann." Now she was whispering so I wouldn't shush her. There was enough rush of noisy air coming from our mouths to have launched a hot air balloon. "I want you to see something."

We pushed open the door and there was only one Quality woman in the place. She was washing her hands and tucking her hair up. She licked one finger and pushed up her eyebrow. Then she licked another finger and pushed up the other one. Anyone could tell that she was a good, clean woman since she didn't lick the same finger to do the other brow. She was certainly a lesson in Quality. Watching Quality at her toilette was not, however, what Mama had in mind. When the lady left, after giving a good tug at her girdle, we went to the first booth. The toilet seat was dry! We made every stall, eight of them, and — they were all dry!

Mama said, "See, Joyce Ann." I shook my head in amazement and agreement, but never till the day she died did I ever have the courage to ask an explanation about the dry toilet seats. The only logical conclusion was that Quality women took a better aim.

Being a High Toned Woman constituted a career of sorts for country women. The career offered many opportunities, good working conditions, selected hours, and executive positions only, but the pay was poor and chances for advancement were limited. After woman's oldest profession, and woman's second-oldest profession of motherhood, being a High Toned Woman might qualify as a woman's third-oldest profession.

There was one rare opportunity for a High Toned Woman to advance in the world, unlike women in the first two professions. She could become a missionary. It seemed in my child's mind that every missionary I ever met was female and High Toned. That truth, of course, did not everywhere abound, but we all live by our own assumptions, and for all I knew, to be female was a requirement to being a missionary. What little we knew of geography or the larger world, we knew from mission study. God called upon missionaries and us to feed the hungry and to clothe the naked. I thought the African people needed our kind of food — corn bread and red beans, chicken fried steak, such as that — and I didn't worry about their getting it because good money went regularly to the mission fund and probably some good missionary prepared it herself around a cozy campfire in the jungle. (Another assumption was that Africans were the only ones who needed missionaries, and that they along with Tarzan and Cheetah had about all the bases covered.) But I could see how the missionaries *needed* help with the clothes. It was a long time, and only after repeated trips to the forbidden *National Geographic*, that I realized that the heathen Africans preferred nakedness and the missionaries preferred to have them cover their nakedness. The logic was clear. You couldn't have naked, brown humans running around disrobed in front of a High Toned Woman. I nearly wept when the truth sank in. Clothing the naturally naked was the high aim of the missionary movement before 1950. Such a work! To be able to gather barrels of clothes so that all Africans, every last naked one of them, might sweat, itch, and pull at tight underwear as I did was worthy of my best efforts. I could help civilize and robe them in a fashion worthy to be presented at the throne of God. I wanted to see every last God's one of them cinched, girded about the loins, trussed up, and covered with Fruit of the Loom, not merely a fig leaf. Putting clothes on Adam and Eve was almost the first civilized act of God when the pair brought sin and civilization upon themselves, and I intended to make it my life's work by way of the U.S. mail. Wisdom was a long, long time in coming, and if in my mind I had to undress as many Africans as I had sworn to clothe, the job would not have been too great.

If it seems that High Toned Women were found consorting in merely busy business of predominantly religious affairs, it should be pointed out that the same women had a goodness about them unequaled in any period of history. These same women were the ones trusted to hold a dying child, called upon to console a widow, asked to bear sad news in a telegram which no woman should have to read from paper, relied upon to prepare graves, and honored for remembering all the proper rituals of the heart which have never been written down. If they were the authorities in matters of living, they were also the ones enduring enough to accompany us to the edge of the grave and to bring us back again to the land of the living, drawing us after them in footsteps plainly visible. Trained psychologists and psychiatrists would only wonder at the wisdom, the deftness in dealing with the human condition, the splendid appropriateness of their gestures and their words. The professionals should reach back in time and call them "sister."

But there is more: gifts of food, little surprises for the children they knew, gifts for acquaintances; they were peacemakers in family and community. The positive force which emanated from High Toned Women made many of them eligible for sainthood.

I do believe that the clan, High Toned, is universal and occurs in all civilizations from pagan to Christian, from Africa to South America, from Siberia to Australia, and represents a kind of feminine category peculiar to every nationality on earth. Somebody ought to fund a salary and give a professorship, free research assistants, and living accommodations to any writer who would hunt and write about the High Toned Woman. (They did all that for James A. Michener and he didn't even find out that there was such a creature in this incomparable state.)

The status and importance of High Toned Women were probably felt only in female domains. Males, as far as I could see, paid no attention to them unless perhaps a preacher had to deal with them from time to time. There does not appear to be a related category known as High Toned Men, for instance. No one questioned a woman's role

"I'm perfectly agreeable to a 50-50 relationship. You make the money and I'll spend it."

in male relationships either. It was usually a woman-to-woman thing. How women kept house may have been of some interest, but how they performed in the bedroom was a question peculiar only to 1970 and after, and by then High Toned Women were all gone. Most men probably felt like Ernie Ford, knowing that no High Toned Woman would make them walk the line — maybe.

The decline of High Toned Women began with World War II when women went to work and opened up a whole new classification of types. Radio, which brought the voices of the nation and the world into the living room, did no favor for High Toned Women. Movies occasionally captured one or two on film, but High Toned Women were always featured in supporting roles, which is, perhaps, what High Toned Women did best — support. Movies make of them merely Busy Bodies. The Andy Hardy series comes to mind. Aunt

Bee in the Andy Griffin television series approached High Toned, but fell short, too. It could be that Schick centers took up High Toned Women's work, and Dear Abby is a close confidant as modern women can find. Barbara Walters asks questions that real High Toned Women avoided at all costs. When there is no need, High Toned Women, or any other institutions of folklore, pass away, and new forms of popular culture rise to fill the gap. I'm not sure they have been replaced with "something of value."

I shall gladly help bury the High Toned Woman with tenderness, care, and sweet remembrance, but let no one say that I helped dig her grave. Do not forget the type. Go to some exotic, strange, remote, primitive, backward, rural timeless place, if you can find it, and you will still find the High Toned Woman. She may not speak your language, but you will know her when you see her. If you would, perhaps, care to form a club, please meet me later. I am already the president, and so you need not apply for that job. And just as soon as I can get my corset laced and my hymnbook out, we shall stand outside on the corner and sing the anthem of High Toned Women, always done as a solo, "The Ninety and Nine," the last verse of which goes:

> And all through the mountains thunder river
> And up from the rocky steep
> There arose a glad cry from the gates of heaven
> Rejoice I have found my sheep
> And the angels echoed around the throne
> Rejoice for the Lord brings back his own.
> Rejoice for the Lord brings back his own.

Printed with permission from Joyce Gibson Roach
Hoein' the Short Rows
Edited by Francis Edward Abernathy
Publication of Texas Folklore Society
University of North Texas Press
1987

Perhaps men should think twice before making widowhood our only path to power.

Gloria Steinem

"I knew you'd like it."

Q: How should you respond to a friend who asks a favor of you on his deathbed when you have no intentions of carrying out the favor after his death?
A: "You'll have to speak up...I still can't hear you...Pardon?...Oh damn! Nurse, I think my friend is dead."

Patricia Marx
Excerpts from *You Can Never Go Wrong By Lying*
Reprinted by permission of Houghton Mifflin Company
Text copyright (c) 1985 by Patricia Marx

The woman is life, and the man is the servant of life.

Epitaph

(Said to have been found in
Bushey Churchyard, Hertfordshire)

HERE lies a poor woman who always was tired,
For she lived in a place where help wasn't hired,
Her last words on earth were, 'Dear friends, I am going.
Where washing ain't done nor cooking nor sewing,
And everything there is exact to my wishes,
For there they don't eat, there's no washing of dishes,
I'll be where loud anthems will always be ringing
(But having no voice, I'll be out of the singing).
Don't mourn for me now, don't grieve for me never,
For I'm going to do nothing for ever and ever.'

                                                    Anonymous

———————

Male hostility to women is a constant; all men hate all
women some of the time, some men hate some women all
of the time. Unfortunately, women cannot bring themselves
to hate men, possibly because they carry them in their
womb from time to time.

                    Gloria Greer
                    The Back Lash Myth in the New
                    Republic
                    October 5, 1992

———————

When Golda Meir became Israel's minister for Foreign
Affairs, a reporter asked her how it felt to be a female
minister. She replied, "I don't know, I've never been a male
foreign minister."

                    Golda Meir
                    1956

———————

Q: How should you act if you never received an invitation to
a wedding you were orally invited to and then run into the
couple a few days before the event?

A: Ask them if they ever got your present (that you never sent).

Patricia Marx
Excerpts from *You Can Never Go Wrong By Lying*
Reprinted by permission of Houghton Mifflin Company
Text Copyright (c) 1985 by Patricia Marx

GEO. CRENSHAW

"Well, make up your mind...you wanna speak to the head of the house, or my daddy?"

A Terrible Infant

I recollect a nurse call'd Ann,
    Who carried me about the grass,
And one fine day a fine young man
    Came up, and kiss'd the pretty lass.
She did not make the least objection!
    Thinks I, '*Aha!*
When I can talk I'll tell Mamma'
    — And that's my earliest recollection.

Frederick Locker-Lampson
1821-1895

I must tell you that I married Mr. Right. I just didn't know that his first name was Always.

Three and a Half Husbands

What is a smile worth? No one can calculate its value. My Aunt Molly had a smile that enchanted everyone. It lit up not only her face but the room where she was sitting. The gods have been good to Aunt Molly, because she had a wealth of auburn hair with a touch of gold and a wide mouth with very white teeth and that wonderful smile. Her skin was white and her figure like an hourglass, and she used that figure effectively whenever a male was near, moving as sinuously as a cat. Her theory was that males respond with ardor to a female if she reveals that she is a womanly woman, and my Aunt Molly was the epitome of femaleness in all its dimensions: sex lure, tenderness, willfulness, courage and originality. Her eyes were made to flutter with a come-on look; her hands white and soft, to be held; her throat, to be kissed; and her lips to promise sweetness.

She was my favorite relative and fascinated me with her ideas. For example, she once worked in a blouse factory, but she hated going to work. She explained that this was because she had to get up early in the morning, which did not agree with her.

"Hold it — That's perfect!"

"For me to get up in the morning," she insisted, "is not good." Her theory was that the morning sun was best for sleep. "That's when your strength and health are fortified," she told me.

"Where did you get that idea?" I asked her. I had never heard that any scientist had done research on such a possibility.

My Aunt Molly looked at me with patience. "I should wait for a scientist to tell me what I know! I know what I know." And having decided that her theory was fact, Aunt Polly operated as though it were a law of nature.

Aunt Molly also decided that the only way she could sleep late in the morning was to quit her job and get married. Finding a husband was no problem.

She had merely to smile her ravishing smile, undulate her sinuous body, heave her magnificent breasts, and the male she had set after had no chance — caught by her loveliness and coquetry.

The most available male for Molly at the time was the superintendent of the blouse factory. He had as much chance of escaping as the fly in the spider's web. That Bill was a widower with three young sons didn't worry Aunt Molly. My mother, Molly's sister, was the one who did the worrying.

"Molly, three boys," she warned, "are not easy to take care of. That's worse than a job! What do you know about boys?"

"So, what do I have to know about boys?" argued Molly. "They should wash their faces, go to school, do their home-work. Do I have to take a course about boys? Foolishness, Bertha!"

So Aunt Molly wore a diamond and a wedding band and could sleep as late as she liked; and Bill, the superintendent of the blouse factory, once again had a wife, and his three boys had a mother; and we had all the blouses we could wear, because Aunt Molly's philosophy was that an aunt should not go visiting empty-handed. From that time on we had blouses coming out of our ears — at least a three-year supply. And Aunt Molly grew more beautiful, as if to prove her point that the morning sun was good for one's health.

For three months Molly had her morning hours of sleep. Bill, the superintendent, was bewildered by Molly, her loveli-ness and her ideas; and the three boys were awed. But then, suddenly, it was all over, for Bill mistook the elevator door at the factory for an office door and fell down the eleva-tor shaft. Molly was left a widow, the blouses ended, the three boys were once again orphaned, and Aunt Molly gave up her sunlit morning sleep and went back to her old job.

But she still had her swaying figure and her smile, the beautiful hair curled around her throat, and her laugh, the laugh of a radiant woman. Men still pursued her. This time it was the custodian of the building who fell for her.

"I know," she said, "I should wait a year, but it's too much to take care of the three boys alone."

My mother was aghast. "Three months ago Bill died, and already she is talking of marriage. What kind of a sister have I got? What will the neighbors say?"

"I think they should say," I told my mother, "that my Aunt Molly is wonderful. Who else would take three orphaned boys? She could send them to an orphan asylum, but Aunt Molly said, 'I should die first. Such nice boys, and they look at me with such frightened eyes.'

"'What will you do with us, Aunt Molly?' they ask.

"'What will I do with you? They should live so long who say that I should give you up. You will stay with me.'"

So Aunt Molly got another diamond ring and married Al, the custodian of the factory. And though there were no more blouses, the custodian had a carriage, and when he and Molly came to visit, we knew that we now had a rich aunt and that Molly had gone back to sleeping late in the morning.

A few months after Molly married Al, his sister died and left a son, Douglas, twelve years old. Aunt Molly brought the orphan home and informed Bill's three sons that they would all have to help take care of him.

I thought my mother would have a nervous breakdown.

"Molly, four boys! You are out of your mind!"

"What difference does it make? One more or less is of no consequence."

But alas, Al was repairing something on top of the building and fell off the roof and broke his neck, leaving Aunt Molly widowed once more — now with four children.

A settlement was made by the owners of the building, from which Molly received $3,500. This time Aunt Molly was really rich, so she bought herself a house and a beautiful black outfit. A friend learned about Molly and came to see her. "I've got the man for you. He is a widow with five children, all boys."

Aunt Molly turned white. "Five more boys!" she exclaimed.

"So what?" said her friend. "Five — seven — eleven. What difference does it make? He's got a good job. He is a superintendent in a beer plant.

"No," protested Aunt Molly. "I had one superintendent. I should take another one? And please, don't bother me with your proposal."

"All right, all right, who's forcing you? But would it hurt to look at him? Looking doesn't cost any money, and if you

would like him, you can look again. If you don't, you can
send me a bill for forcing you to meet him. So, is that a
good arrangement?"

After all, Aunt Molly did have the new outfit. And she
had not been married to either of her two husbands long
enough to feel any grief, so she let herself be persuaded to
meet the beer superintendent.

Aunt Molly married again, and now there were nine boys
in her household, all noisy and boisterous and healthy, and
all learning to love Aunt Molly.

Aunt Molly's marriage to Sol, her third husband, lasted
less than two years, for Sol contracted pneumonia and died
within two weeks. Aunt Molly, normally vivacious and cheerful, begun to believe that hers was a strange fate.

She was distraught. "Why would God do this to me?
Who else in the whole world's buried three husbands in five
years? What does God mean by this?"

The nine boys surrounded her. "Aunt Molly, don't you
cry," they pleaded, but as she wept, they all began to weep,
too. What could anyone say?

"How does it happen," Molly asked my mother, "that other
women marry and stay married for forty and fifty years but I
lose my husbands right away?"

In the midst of her tears she noticed her hat. It was
brown. She needed a black hat. No one in the family had
one.

"But why, Aunt Molly? What difference does it make
whether you wear a black hat or a brown one? What earthly
difference can it possibly make?" I asked.

"Do you hear that, Bertha, what your daughter is saying?
What difference will it make? I should go to the funeral of
my third husband and wear a brown hat? If it were my first
husband or even my second, but for the third? How would it
look if I wore a brown hat, I ask you," she demanded.

There was no use arguing with Aunt Molly. A black hat
she would have to have.

Kenneth, one of Molly's first husband's sons, said, "All
right, Aunt Molly, you will have a black hat," and he proceeded to haul out his liquid black shoe polish. He covered Aunt

Molly's brown straw with the black polish and then presented it to her.

"What about these?" asked Aunt Molly, indicating the white flowers on the hat.

"Give it back," said Kenneth, and he proceeded to paint the flowers black.

"Now," I said to Molly, "you've ruined the hat. Where else can you wear it?"

"With Molly's luck her fourth husband will die, and she will have a hat ready," my mother said.

At this, Aunt Molly rose from her chair and addressed all of us. "You should all listen to me and hear what your Aunt Molly has to say. You, Kenneth, who are the eldest, and Robert and Douglas. And you, my sister; and you, my brother, Sam. And you, my niece" — turning to me. "On this day I call on God to listen to me. I know what God wants. Maybe He doesn't speak to me like he did to Moses, but this is not the ancient times. But He spoke to me. 'Molly,' He said, 'you are not ever to get married again, because whoever you marry will die.' I am telling all of you — my sons, my niece, my sister and brother — no more marriages for me."

We were silenced. It was true that Sol was Molly's third husband and that each one of them had died before the end of the second year of their marriage. To hold God responsible for their deaths, that we could understand; but to say that God doomed Molly and that for some inscrutable reason known only to the Deity any man she married was doomed to die soon afterward — this left us all in consternation.

My mother said, "Another Moses. And when did you speak to God that you know all of this?"

By this time Molly was wringing her handkerchief. "To you He would have to speak. But to me, He doesn't have to use words. Am I such a fool that I don't understand Him? Tell me, if you are smart, who else do you know who has buried three husbands? Mrs. Ginsburg's husband lost a foot. They had to cut it off. Did he die? No, he wears a false foot. Mrs. Epstein's husband had pneumonia. Did he die? The doctors gave him up, but what does Mr. Epstein do? He gets better! But me, Molly, has buried three husbands in five years. When my Sol got sick, the doctor said, 'Don't worry, he'll be all right.' But my Sol isn't Mr. Epstein. As soon as the doctor left, what does my Sol do — he opens his eyes and says, 'Coffee, Molly,' and dies. Whoever heard of a husband asking for coffee and then dying? Who else do you know? Whoever heard of such a thing that a man with two eyes that can see should fall down an elevator shaft? Why in all the United States of America does my Bill have to step into an elevator that isn't there? You tell me why?"

"But, Molly," remonstrated her brother-in-law, "other husbands die. You are not the only one who loses a husband."

Molly turned to him. "Sure, sure, I know other husbands die, but if you are so smart, tell me one other woman who you know who has lost three husbands."

We were again silenced.

"You see, there is a curse on me. I'll wear this hat this time, to the funeral, and I'll never wear it again, because I'll never marry again."

"You shouldn't talk so silly," said Sam. "You are not God."

"So, I'm not God, but I won't get married, and I'll take care of the nine boys, and I'll be a father and mother to them."

Her family protested, "Molly, nine boys — you'll go crazy."

"So," said Molly, "what should I do with them? Throw them out on the street? I'm a rich woman now. Bill left me $5,000 in his will; Al, 3,500; and Sol, 8,000. On $16,500 the boys and I will live."

Kenneth, the oldest, was thirteen, and the youngest, Michael, was three. In the early 1900s, $16,500 was a lot of money, but the family warned her that she would have trouble with the boys.

"Me?" said Molly, "I've had trouble — three husbands — God has done enough to me. I've agreed no matter what — no more husbands. So, God should please let me alone." She always talked about God as though He were a relative and they had a direct line of communication.

Aunt Molly was sad and silent. Her violet-blue eyes with their long lashes, were often filled with tears. With nine boys it was imperative that she get a job. Nothing could persuade her to give up the boys. "No," she said, "they are mine and God wants me to keep them." There was no use in arguing with Molly about God.

"Aunt Molly," I suggested, "you will get married again."

"So, tell me who would marry me with nine children?"

"Molly, they are not your responsibility. Their relatives should care for them."

"Responsibility, schmonsibility!" was Molly's retort. "Of course they are mine. Sol wouldn't rest in his grave if he thought they were not with me." And then she repeated, "I'm not ever going to get married again, because if I do, the man will die."

"Nonsense," my mother responded, "why should he die?"

"Well," asked Aunt Molly, "if you are so smart, why did three of them die? They were alive until they married me."

My mother gave up arguing with her. But when Aunt Molly said she wouldn't marry anyone, she didn't mean she would be without a man. That was a life too bleak for her. She met other custodians and other superintendents; she wouldn't marry them. They could be her lovers, but no marriage. She had developed a real phobia about marriage, and nothing could sway her.

At one time, the man of the moment was the owner of a butcher shop. She explained that, in her position, it was good to be friendly with the owner of a food store because there were nine boys to feed.

After a year, her butcher friend contracted pneumonia but recovered, and Molly triumphantly pointed out that this was proof that she was right. He didn't die — he survived. If she had been married to him, she knew, he would have died. Who could argue with such logic?

After the butcher recovered, she lost interest in him. It was as though she had proved her point and had no further use for him, or perhaps it was because there was someone new on the horizon. This time it was an osteopath. We didn't know what an osteopath was, so we looked up the

word in the dictionary — and Aunt Molly took on added
stature. But the osteopath didn't last long; the boys didn't
like him, and that really influenced Aunt Molly.

Aunt Molly had ideas of her own about how to bring up
the boys and how the insurance money should be spent.

The oldest of the nine boys, Kenneth, was thirteen.
Molly lined them all up, from the three-year-old to the thir-
teen-year-old, and made a speech.

"I am now," she said, "both your father and your mother.
The insurance money will be put away for the three oldest
boys' college education; then those three will work and pro-
vide the money for the younger ones' educations. We will
all," she said, "sign such an agreement."

I still have that agreement among my cherished possessions. That agreement reads, "I, Molly Davidson, promise to
raise Kenneth, Michael, Robert, Douglas, Donald, Victor,
Jonas, Isadore, and Irwin. From this day, June 12, 1903,
they will be my true sons and they will educate each other.
When the first one is finished with college, he will help the
next one. I want for each to be a doctor or a writer or a
lawyer or an engineer, but no superintendents. So, help me,
God. Signed, Molly Davidson."

Her signature was followed by that of all the boys except
Michael, who drew a circle, since he was too young to write.

Bill had bought a large house, with six bedrooms, so
Molly easily made room for all the boys. She had some of
them double up and allocated the largest room to the three
youngest. The attic was a storeroom for their possessions,
and the basement accommodated some of their activities —
practicing on the trombone and their violins and Jonas' wood
carving. In the dining room, there was a table big enough
for fourteen. Molly always had the meals in the dining room;
the kitchen wasn't big enough for all nine and herself.
Washing the linens each week, and the boys' shirts and
socks, was a job, but Mrs. Kolensky, a widow, was hired to
do the housework.

The house rang with singing and laughter. Sometimes
Molly thought how nice it would be to have a quiet house,
but mostly she adjusted to the boys' boisterous hours, for

she felt peace within herself. It was her atonement to the three husbands who had died so prematurely, as if it were her fault. Somehow she felt she had not loved them enough. At least she would care for her sons.

The bathroom was the real problem, but Molly was equal to all problems. A schedule was made out allocating five minutes each morning for washing and brushing teeth, and the time for each of the boys was pasted up in the bathroom. Bathing, also, was listed — two for Monday night, two for Tuesday, and so on. The basin and the tub had to be left spotless for the next in line.

Molly dreamed of having a second bathroom. A bathroom for herself with a place for her perfume, her cosmetics and her trinkets. Molly was sybaritical. She loved beautiful things around her. She rejoiced in dresses that swished as she moved. Frequently she used one kind of perfume on her skirt and another kind on her blouse. Her three husbands had had good incomes and had indulged her tastes. "They could afford it."

Because she had worked in the blouse factory before her marriage, and earned only a small wage, the luxury her husbands had planned for her was intoxicating. She reveled in her new opulence. And conscious of what she owed them, she transferred to their sons her sense of obligation to the three husbands.

The boys knew that Molly wanted a second bathroom, so they saved their money, and by Christmas they were proud owners of $37.19. They presented the money with great solemnity to Molly and told her that now she could have her second bathroom.

So Molly had a new bathroom installed, which was known as the Christmas bathroom. Further, the boys told Aunt Molly that it was to be her own exclusive bathroom. Molly cried.

"Aunt Molly, aren't you pleased?"

"Of course, but you should know my heart hurts when I am happy."

"Oh well," exclaimed Irwin, one of the twins and thus the second eldest, "maybe Aunt Molly's heart is different than other people's."

Aunt Molly did take care of the boys, and it was something to see all of them sitting at the table. She never brought them all to our house at one time, because there wouldn't have been enough room. How those boys worked! They peddled papers; they ran errands for the neighbors; they worked at the butcher shop; they helped the janitor at school. And they pooled their money. There was only one bicycle, and each boy had an assigned day to use it.

On report card day, Aunt Molly would sit and solemnly scrutinize each card before signing her name. The devotion of all the boys to one another was remarkable. No fights at school without the whole gang defending one another. They were known as The Davidson Gang and had no trouble. No one attacked any one of them, because if anyone did, the whole group would turn on him.

Molly had a unique method of bringing up the boys. Douglas, Molly's son by courtesy of Al, her Episcopalian husband, was a quiet boy of twelve given to reading everything he could lay his hands on. Molly would sometimes say to him, "Douglas, come back from wherever you are; you have to live in this world. What's the matter, honey boy? Don't you like this world? Stop reading so many books. I don't want you to be like the Goldberg boy. He reads so much he has to wear double glasses."

If she had a favorite, it was Douglas; for he was a reflective child, but he was not shy. When there was something that he was interested in or wanted, he would sturdily defend his position. While he was still twelve he informed Aunt Molly that he was not going to go to Sunday school any longer.

"Why?" asked Molly. "All nice boys go to Sunday school. What will the neighbors think if you don't go?"

"I won't go," said Douglas, "because I don't believe in God."

This stumped Molly. "How can a little boy like you say he doesn't believe in God?" she asked.

"What has my size got to do with it?" retorted Douglas. "My brain is just as big as Kenneth's, and he's thirteen."

"You see,' said Aunt Molly triumphantly, "that's what becomes of all of this book business. Your nose is always stuck in some book."

"Well," asserted Douglas, "I don't believe in Him, so I'm not going. Besides, our Sunday school teacher is a dope and her nose is always red."

"So," said Molly, "we'll get you a teacher with a white nose."

"I'm not going," Douglas persisted.

"Listen to the little punk," said Kenneth. "Who do you think you are saying you're not going to Sunday school?"

"Just your little brother," said Douglas. "And what's more, you can talk — you don't have to go."

"Well, I did, didn't I; and wasn't I confirmed?"

But Molly was a pragmatist. She knew that the neighbors would talk if one of the boys didn't go to Sunday school. They would hold her sinful ways responsible. So she tried another tack with Douglas. "All right, you don't believe in God. Do you have to tell the whole world? Did they ask you if you believed in Moses and the Disciples and all the other Biblical figures? No one asked you. So, why can't you go as a favor to me? I'll give you a dime every Sunday for going."

The dime was too much for Douglas. It was a munificent sum to receive every week, so he yielded. "All right, just so you understand I don't believe in all that dribble," warned Douglas.

This was too much for the other boys. "Why should he get a dime for going to Sunday school?" They didn't.

Molly said, "Well, it's easier for you, because Douglas is an Episcopalian, and his religion is harder to understand and believe than yours."

Dorothy Fuldheim
Three and a Half Husbands
John Carroll University, Cleveland
1976

"Yoo-hoo, dear, still mad at me?"

First Woman: "I got this bottle of Scotch for my mother-in-law."
Second Woman: "Holy smokes...what a trade!"

Q: Does it count to send someone a Christmas card in lieu of a letter you owe?
A. It counts for Hallmark, not for you.

> Patricia Marx
> *You Can Never Go Wrong By Lying*
> Houghton Mifflin Publishing Co.
> 1985

Reflections at Dawn

I wish I owned a Dior dress
   Made to my order out of satin.
I wish I weighed a little less
   And could read Latin,
Had perfect pitch or matching pearls,
   A better head for sweet directions,
And seven daughters, all with curls
   And fair complexions.
I wish I'd tan instead of burn.
   But most, on all the stars that glisten,
I wish at parties I could learn
   To sit and listen.

I like two kinds of men: domestic and foreign.

                 Mae West

Q: What can you give a friend who has everything?
A: Shelves.

        Patricia Marx
        Excerpts from *You Can Never Go*
        Wrong By Lying
        Reprinted by permission of Houghton
        Mifflin Company
        Text copyright (c) 1985 by Patricia
        Marx

Footnote to Tennyson

I feel it when the game is done,
I feel it when I suffer most.
'Tis better to have loved and lost
Than ever to have loved and won.

              Gerald Bullett

Q: How does a man prove he's planning for the future?
A: He buys two cases of beer and not one.

———>●<———

Sometimes you just can't win. Consider this woman futiley trying to move in and out of a parking space. A guy saw her and tried to help, motioning her first this way and then that way until she was safely in the parking space. Then she said, "Thanks so much for your help, sir, but I was trying to move out of this space, not into it."

———>●<———

How is a man like the weather? Nothing can be done to change either of them.

———>●<———

A young lady who had been hired by a large supermarket chain reported to work at one of the stores. The manager greeted her with a warm handshake and a smile, then handed her a broom and said: "Your first job will be to sweep out the store."

"But," the young woman said, "I'm a college graduate."

"Oh, excuse me," the manager replied, "I didn't know that. Here, give me the broom and I will show you how."

———>●<———

Q: What's the difference between men and hogs?
A: Hogs don't turn into men when they drink.

———>●<———

Auntie

Auntie always was morose
And her views on life were bitter,
For she was so adipose

No ordinary scat would fit'er:
Now I should think that you'd feel glum
If you'd been born with Auntie's sitter!

Anonymous

—————>●<—————

Furniture is the other thing a wife likes to push around.

—————>●<—————

Q: When should you walk out of a movie?
A: When you realize that your watch is more interesting than the movie.

Patricia Marx
Excerpts from *You Can Never Go Wrong By Lying*
Reprinted by permission of Houghton Mifflin Company
Text copyright (c) 1985 by Patricia Marx

—————>●<—————

My wife calls our water bed the "Dead Sea."

Milton Berle

—————>●<—————

The Smart Husband and the Smarter Wife

Once there lived in Cowplain in Connecticut a God-fearing fellow named Josiah, who was rich in goods of the world. He had a fine house and he had fat cows; he had a strong horse and much money; but best of all he had a good head on his shoulders and could think out things proper.

One Sunday after church he was sitting in his high-backed chair by the fireside thinking about this and that, when a thought he'd never had before came to his mind. Spoke he to himself as was ever his wont:

GEORGE
CRENSHAW

"I've all man kin desire, and I'm greatly blessed and happy indeed. I'm so happy, I'm feared when my time comes fer me to go to Heaven in a chariot I'll be loath to leave. Nay, I know for certain I'll be unhappy. An' I don't wish to be unhappy ever. I must do somethin' 'bout this."

Thereupon he thought again for a long time and spoke again to himself:

"Now, here is a good thought. Perhaps if I had some honest trouble in life jest as my neighbors, I'd be glad to go to Heaven instead of bein' sorry."

Then he thought again for a long time and spoke again to himself:

"When I meet my friends in the tavern they all speak more 'bout the trouble they have wi' wives than any trouble ever with horses or cows. It'd seem to me if I got me a wife I'd have troubles, too, so when my time comes to go to Heaven I'll be pretty glad to do so. And since I'm the most contented man in Cowplain near Cedar Mountain, I must get me the worst wife to make certain I'll have plenty o' trouble."

The next morning he set out and traveled up and down the roads of Connecticut to find the worst wife he could find. He also looked in on Cabul Hill, Hang Dog, and Vexation Hill. Though he looked everywhere, he couldn't find the right kind of wife he sought. So he turned home again.

When he came to the first meadow and passed by Andrus' house, his nearest neighbor, he heard a screaming and screeching to split the ears. That was Hannah, Andrus' only daughter, whom none would marry, for she was the crossest creature in all the state. She'd argue, and nip and nag friends and neighbors, just for the sake of arguing, nipping, and nagging. Truth to tell, she was the worst woman in all the land.

"Thanks unto the Lord! That's the wife for me," Josiah cried joyfully. "And she was right near by all the time while I was a-lookin' for her all over the land."

He rode quickly right up to the door and knocked loudly. But they heard him not for the scolding and screaming. So he knocked harder, and the door flung open wide. Hannah stood there, with brown-red hair flying in all directions like frightened sparrows, and eyes blazing paths of dark lightning.

"An' what brings you here?" she cried angrily.

"It's the Lord's will that ye marry me, Hannah," said Josiah.

Hannah caught her breath quicker than a jack rabbit running and pinched herself sideways to make sure she wasn't dreaming. No man had ever spoken such words to her before, let alone one so rich as Josiah. Then her answer jumped out of her mouth:

"The Lord's will be done, Josiah."

So the two were wedded, and things went well indeed. Hannah made plenty of trouble and it looked as if Josiah would gladly go any time to Heaven without feeling sorry to leave.

One evening he was sitting on a bench with Sled and Hunn, his two best friends, and some other men, in front of the green, and one queried him how he fared with Hannah.

Said Josiah, "Faith, it couldn't be better, She scolds the day long, never givin' me no peace. It's just what I want her to do."

"Now that is a strange thing for a husband to want," said Sled.

"I'd like to know why ye married the worst shrew that ever was?" asked Hunn.

"I'll tell you why, friend Hunn," spoke Josiah. "I had every joy a man kin want on this earth, and I was afeared when my time came to go to Heaven in a chariot I'd be sorry to leave Cowplain. So I figured I'd be less sorry if I had some trouble just like you and all the others have. Now I've plenty o' trouble. I couldn't find a worse wife in all our great land, yet I'm not complaining, the contrary, I am pleased."

Hunn and Sled and all the others listened, ears big as elephants', and since Hunn was a great gossip, it wasn't long before all Cowplain knew the tale — and Hannah heard it, too.

She was sitting with some womenfold in her home roasting apples, busy at stitching a long sampler and talking gossip while the menfolk were at the tavern talking politics.

Said Abagail, who had been Hannah's friend for years: "I never did expect such a thing from Josiah, though I knew he wasn't silly love-cracked. Know you what he said? He said he married you so you'd make his life so miserable he'd gladly go to Heaven in a chariot when his time came around. He said if life on earth were too pleasurable and without trouble he'd never want to leave it."

"Josiah said 'twas the Lord's will that I marry him," cried Hannah stoutly.

"So he said," spoke another. "So he said, but it had a different meaning from what you thought. He didn't tell you all. But he told it to my husband Hunn. He said that he married you so you'd bring him trouble and he'd be mighty glad indeed to leave this earth."

Hannah was madder that a cat tied in a sack. She fumed and raved, ranted and screamed, telling all the womenfolk what she'd do to her husband when he came home that night.

All of a sudden she ceased her ranting and stood silent for a long time. A smile came slowly to her face, such as was never there before since the day she was born. Her smile grew bigger and bigger, and all the women looked at her in great surprise.

"Good friends," she cried pleasantly, "I'll cheat my husband in his hopes. I'll be no packhorse to carry him to Heaven. You just wait and see!" Then she laughed most pleasantly, a thing she'd never done before.

When Josiah came home that night he wasn't certain he'd come to the right place. Instead of scolding and crying, Hannah greeted him with a loud kiss. Moreover, she was kind and good as she'd never been. And her goodness and kindness never ceased.

From that day on Josiah had the finest wife in all the land, and that put the poor man to great worries. 'Twas not what he'd bargained for. It gave him no peace of mind, and for days he thought on't.

Then one day, while he was walking behind his oxen, digging a furrow in the ground, a truly good thought came to him. A happy smile spread on his face, and he spoke to himself as was ever his wont:

"Why, I'll feel no sorrow to leave this earth when my proper times comes round — if Hannah comes wi' me. She kin sit next to me in the chariot and make my life as pleasant in Heaven as she has on earth!"

From that day on he never worried again and lived happily to the end of his life.

As for Hunn, who tried to make trouble for Josiah, this was writ on his tomb when he left this earth:

"The flesh and bones of Samuel Hunn,
Lie underneath this tomb.
Oh let them rest in quietness
Until the day of Doom."

M. Jagendorf
New England Bean Pot
Vanguard Press, New York
1948

"And do you, Figby, promise to take out the garbage?"

Q: Why don't male lobsters share with their females?
A: Because they are shellfish.

Money isn't everything. If it was, what would we buy with it?

Tom Wilson

The old guy was an egotist and self-assured that he was always a hit with women. In a restaurant, one day, the pretty waitress appealed to him and he said to her: "Where have you been all the years of my life?"

"As a matter of fact, sir," she replied, "I wasn't even around the first forty-five of them."

The wife of a nice elderly couple in Chatham, Illinois visited the doctor for an examination. On the way home she told hubby, "The doctor says I have the heart of a fifty-year-old, the lungs of a thirty-year-old, and have the blood pressure of a twenty-year-old."

"Really?" responded her husband, "and what did he say about your seventy-year-old ass?"

She replied: "He never mentioned your name."

———>●<———

Man: He who rules the roost.
Woman: She who rules the rooster.

———>●<———

If sex is so personal, why are we expected to share it with somebody else?

Lily Tomlin

———>●<———

A little girl was going around the neighborhood raising money for her girl scout troop. She knocked on the door of one house and a man opened the door, heard her request and invited her in. She sat in the living room and the man came over and put a dollar bill beside a dime on the table beside her and said, "Now take your choice."

The little girl picked up both saying, "I'll wrap the dime in the dollar bill so I can take it home safely."

———>●<———

A smart husband is one who thinks twice and then says nothing.

———>●<———

The little girl said to her mother: "I wish you'd let me take my bath in the morning before school instead of at night before bed."

"But why?" Mother asked. "What's the difference?"

"Here's why. Every day at school the teacher tells us kids that everybody who had a bath today should stand up. I haven't been able to stand since school started."

Woman to the marriage counselor: "The only thing we have in common is that we were married on the same day."

———⇒●⇐———

A woman surgeon was disturbed about the high cost of her car repair.

"This is ridiculous!" she said, "charging me five hundred dollars to grind the valves and put in new piston rings."

"Not really, just think about it. You are a surgeon and should know that an automobile engine is just as complicated as a human body. The mechanic who serviced your car is just as skilled as you are."

"Is that so...well, let me see him grind valves while the engine is running."

———⇒●⇐———

My parents have been married for forty years. I asked my mom how they managed it. She said, "You just close your eyes and pretend it never happened."

———⇒●⇐———

Her mother noticed that the bride-to-be was inviting only married friends to her wedding. Disturbed by this, her mother asked why she invited only married friends and the daughter's reply was:

"Well, Mom, if I invited a lot of my unmarried friends, one by one they would marry and I would have to buy them wedding presents. But, this way, inviting only my married friends, all of our presents are clear profit."

A Word to Husbands

To keep your marriage brimming
With love in the loving cup,
Whenever you're wrong, admit it;
Whenever you're right, shut up.

Ogden Nash
Selected Poetry of Ogden Nash

———————

Poise: the ability to continue talking while the other woman picks up the check.

———————

The family was enjoying a meal at a quiet restaurant. But the little boy couldn't finish his steak. So the father called the waiter over and asked for a box to take the remnant steak "home to the dog."

The little boy jumped out of his chair, very excited, and said, "Oh boy! Does that mean we're going to get a puppy?"

———————

Mother rabbit to her little bunny, "A magician pulled you out of a hat! Now stop asking foolish questions!"

———————

Backing out of a car space, the woman hit another car and scratched only her own fender.

"Don't let it bother you," her husband said. "Just take it to the body shop on 8th Street and have them fix it."

But hard luck seemed to dog her because as she backed out of her garage a few days after the damage had been repaired, she hit the side of the garage and tore the rear light off of the car.

"Don't worry about it," said her husband. "Just take it to the same shop and tell them your husband did it. That way you won't embarrass yourself."

"Unfortunately, my dear, I can't do that. That's what I told them the last time I took the car there."

———⇒●⇐———

Are you living a life of quiet desperation or are you married?

———⇒●⇐———

A waste or extravagance is anything you buy that is of no use to your husband.

The Wife

"Home they brought her warrior dead:
She nor swooned, nor uttered cry.
All her maidens, watching, said,
'She must weep, or she will die.'"

The propriety of introducing a sad story like the following, in a book intended to be rather cheerful in its character, may be questioned; but it so beautifully illustrates the firmness of woman when grief and despair have taken possession of "the chambers of her heart," that we cannot refrain from relating it.

Lucy M — loved with all the ardor of a fond and faithful wife, and when he upon whom she had so confidingly leaned was stolen from her by death, her friends and companions said Lucy would go mad. Ah, how little they knew her!

Gazing for the last time upon the clay-cold features of her departed husband, this young widow — beautiful even in her grief; so ethereal to look upon, and yet so firm! — looking for the last time upon the dear familiar face, now cold and still in death — oh, looking for the last, last time — she rapidly put on her bonnet, and thus addressed the sobbing gentlemen who were to act as pall-bearers: — "You pall-bearers, just go into the buttery and get some rum, and we'll start this man right along!"

Artemus Ward
1834-1867

Edith was practicing violin when suddenly there was a heavy pounding on the front door. When she opened it there stood a breathless cop.

"What's wrong?" she asked.

"Where's the body?" the cop asked.

"What on earth are you talking about?" Edith asked.

"We just got a tip that somebody was murdering Beethoven in this house."

Love thy neighbor, but be sure his wife is away first.

———>●<———

A woman had applied for life insurance and the salesman was questioning her. "Have you ever had appendicitis?" he asked.

"Well, I was operated on for it but I was never quite sure whether it was appendicitis or professional curiosity."

———>●<———

"Every time a woman leaves something off she looks better. Every time a man leaves something off he looks worse."

Will Rogers

———>●<———

A woman rushes into the house and yells to hubby, "Paul, pack up your things. I just won the lottery."

Paul replies: "Should I pack for Florida or Alaska?"

The wife replies: "I don't give a hoot, just so long as you're out of here by six o'clock!"

———>●<———

Mary: "Don't you think my birthday cake is a lovely design?"
Sue: "I sure do. Simply lovely...but your arithmetic is awful."

———>●<———

Anyone who remarks that they sleep like a baby, obviously, has never had one.

———>●<———

There are few daughters today that get to use their mother's wedding dress...she's still using it!

Beatrice and Patricia were discussing Patricia's night out with her in-laws. "I don't know what my father-in law does with his money, but I can tell you one thing...he sure doesn't carry it with him when we go out for a drink!"

"I guess you had to pay for the whole meal, right?" asked Beatrice.

"Let me put it this way," responded Patricia, "He is so cheap that he would have asked for separate checks at the last supper."

———————

It's reported that there is a sign just outside a New York night club that reads: "If you drive your man to drink...drive him here!"

———————

Polly: "What's the first thing you would do if you developed a case of hydrophobia?"
Rachel: "I'd ask for a paper and pencil."
Polly: "To make out a will for after your death?"
Rachel: "Nope! To make a list of the guys I want to bite."

———————

Male dentists are the only men in America who can tell women to shut their mouth and not get slapped.

———————

"Samuel, be a good boy and run over to Mrs. Estes house and see how old Mrs. Estes is."

Sammy left to obey his mom's instructions, but soon returned with this announcement: "Mrs. Estes says it's none of your business how old she is!"

Bigamy is having one husband too many...Monogamy is the same thing.

———>≫●≪———

I love him for what he is...wealthy.

———>≫●≪———

A woman had not been feeling well and went to see her doctor to see what was wrong. He gave her a thorough examination and then told her: "Don't smoke anymore, don't drink anymore, and get to bed earlier and up at the crack of dawn. That's the best thing for you."

The woman replied: "Doctor, I don't deserve the best. What's the second best?"

———>≫●≪———

In the window of a fine home in Evanston, Illinois appeared a card announcing "A piano for sale."

In the window next door soon, another card appeared with this word: "Hurrah!"

———>≫●≪———

Sarah: "I'm homesick!"
Millie: "But, dear, don't you live at home?"
Sarah: "I sure do, but I'm sick of it."

CHAPTER FOUR

It's better to be laughed at for not being married than to be unable to laugh because you are.

"There were exercise outfits when I was a girl, too," Grandma said, "Only we called them house dresses."

———⟫●⟪———

Make love, not war, or do both...get married.

———⟫●⟪———

A young mother received a gift of a playpen from her friend. She wrote a note to thank her friend, saying: "I sure do appreciate your wonderful gift. Y'know, I sit in it every afternoon and read. The children can't get even close to me."

———⟫●⟪———

A man in love is incomplete until he's married. Then he's finished.

Zsa Zsa Gabor

———⟫●⟪———

Marrying a man is like buying something you have been admiring for a long time in the shop window. You may love it when you get it home, but it doesn't always go with everything in the house.

MFMMPPMBBLPHMLPF?

"Yes, you were snoring last night."

Married women live a lot longer than single women. But married women are a lot more willing to die.

———————

Q: What's the best way to have your husband recall your wedding anniversary?
A: Get married on his birthday!

———————

A young couple wanted a child very much, but the woman could not get pregnant. Their priest told them he was going to Rome and that he would light a candle there and pray for their success to have a baby.

After being gone for five years, the priest returned and called on the couple. "Did you have any children?" the priest asked the wife.

"You bet, thanks to you. We have five children and will soon have another."

"But where is your husband?" the priest asked.

"He's gone to Rome to put out the candle!" she replied.

———————

The secretary and her boss were having endless arguments. Finally, he said, "If I were your husband, I'd poison you."

His secretary replied, "And if you were my husband, I'd drink it!"

———————

"I hate singles bars. Guys come up to me and say, 'Hey, cupcake, can I buy you a drink?'

I say, "No, but I'll take the three bucks."

Margaret Smith

———————

Little Bobby had been acting up all morning and his mother had spanked him repeatedly. Finally Bobby said, "Mom, give me a dime and I'll be good."

Mom replied, "Why can't you be good for nothing, like your father!"

———————

You know you have reached middle age when the narrow waist and broad mind change places.

———————

"I just returned home from a pleasant trip," Dolly remarked to her neighbor.

"You did? And where did you go?"
"I just drove the kids to school," was the reply.

——————

Marriage is commitment. But, what the heck, so is insanity.

——————

The entire family had come for Christmas dinner to the parents' home.

Before he said grace, the father announced: "I'll give $50,000 to the first in my family to present us with a grandchild." He then bowed his head to pray.

When the prayer was finished, he looked up and only he and his wife were left at the table.

——————

Marriage is bliss. Ignorance is bliss. Therefore...

——————

"Tell me, Mabel," the old lady asked her friend, "How does it feel to be a grandmother?"

"It's sure nice to be a grandmother," was the reply, "But I'm having a hard time getting used to being married to a grandfather."

——————

Marriage is the only game that requires the trapped animal to buy the license.

——————

A few years ago, a woman opened a coffee shop in Chicago. She did everything right from selecting the right spot to adequate advertising, to developing a lovely coffee shop. She didn't make any money. Since not only coffee, but tea, was also a feature of her shop, she discovered that she could save money by using her tea bags from three to four times. And she did...but she went broke — which only proves that "Honest Tea" is the best policy.

———>●<———

Losing a husband can be mighty tough. For me it was almost impossible.

———>●<———

Marriage has been described as a three ring circus: engagement ring, wedding ring, and suffer-ring.

———>●<———

Woman: "I've come to join my husband at the Pearly Gates."
St. Peter: "Good. What's his name?"
Woman: "Willy Jacobs."
St. Peter: "I can't identify him by that common name. Can you give me any more information on him?"
Woman: "Only this. Just before he passed away, he told me that if I ever slept with another guy, he'd turn over in his grave."
St. Peter: "Oh, now I know him. You mean Whirling Willie."

———>●<———

Don't marry for money...you can borrow it cheaper.
                                              Scottish Proverb

———>●<———

A beautiful young Lady-in-Waiting at King Arthur's court sneaked back to her room in the castle and said, "What a knight!"

Did you hear the recent spoonerism? A guy was telling his friend about his new girlfriend. "Her breath will take your beauty away."

—————>◦◦◦<—————

On a boat on Lake Michigan, a young boy fell overboard and was about to be drowned in the rough water. A woman, very well dressed, dived into the water and dragged the boy back to the boat.

The boy's father hugged the woman and said: "You, Ma'am, are a great heroine. How can I ever pay you for what you have done?"

… "Just tell me this, sir," the woman said, "Who pushed me?"

"I want him to look natural. Can you prop him up in a chair and stick a remote in his hand?

After a quarrel, a husband said to his wife: "I was purely a fool to marry you." So, the wife replied: "I know that, but I was in love and didn't notice it."

————⟫●⟪————

Married life can be very frustrating. During the first year, the man speaks and the woman listens; in the second year, the woman speaks and the man listens; but during the third year, they both speak and the neighbors listen.

————⟫●⟪————

Nobody ever forgets where he buried the hatchet.

Kim Hubbard

————⟫●⟪————

The wife of a champion boxer was telling her friend: "It is sure nice to be married to George. Every night he comes home looking like a different person."

————⟫●⟪————

My husband ran off with my friend a few days ago. And, good golly, I sure do miss her.

————⟫●⟪————

A woman returned from a prolonged trip to Europe and was having coffee with friends. A friend asked: "Did you see many poor people, and signs of poverty over there?"

"I sure did," the returnee replied, "And I've brought some of it home with me."

————⟫●⟪————

I require only three things of a man. He must be handsome, ruthless and stupid.

Dorothy Parker

Anne Baxter likes to tell the story of her mother who bought a baby buggy and hired a guy to push Anne around the park every day. And ever since then, Anne has been pushed for money.

———>●<———

Most guys judge a woman based on how she's built. They think the larger the breasts of a woman, the less intelligent she is. But it doesn't really work that way. Rather, it's the larger a woman's breasts are, the less intelligent the men become.

Anita Wise

———>●<———

I want a husband who is good, God-fearing, educated, bright, sincere, respectful of me and treats me as an equal, and has the same interests that I do...So tell me...is that too much to ask of a millionaire?

———>●<———

Jack Parr, the television comedian, used to tell this one: "A guy on my program once told me that his wife fell for every commercial on the air... 'she used five face creams, three chin creams, and even one elbow cream.' I asked the man, "Tell me, how do you keep her from slipping out of bed?"

———>●<———

Did you hear about the Irish immigrant woman who had to visit a chiropodist and told him; "My fate is in your hands."

———>●<———

She had just returned from Russia and was telling her friend about her experiences. "Tell me, dear, have you ever heard of the dance, the Czardas?"
Her friend replied, "That's by Hoagy Carmichael, isn't it?"

Maybelle says that you know you've become middle age when a doctor and not a traffic cop tells you to slow down.

———◦———

A woman executive was asked why she kept a bowl of goldfish in her office. She replied; "I enjoy having something around here that opens its mouth without asking for a raise."

———◦———

First wife: "I hear your husband is a linguist."
Second wife: "He is; he speaks three languages: golf, baseball, and football."

———◦———

After Adam was created in the Garden of Eden, God saw that it was not good for him to be alone; so God said to Adam: "I've got an idea on how to improve your life and relieve your loneliness. I'll give you someone who will make your life complete, take care of you and be a companion to you...but it will cost you at least an arm and a leg. It ain't free."

"That's a very high price, dear God," Adam replied, "What can I get for a rib?"

———◦———

Wife: "If a man or woman steal anything they will live to regret it."
Husband: "You used to steal kisses from me before we were married."
Wife: "Well..."

———◦———

After church one Sunday, a little boy asked his mother: "Mommy, is it true that we are made of dust?"
"Yes, dear."

"And do we turn to dust when we die?"

"Yes, sweetie."

"Well, Mommy, last night after my prayers, I looked under my bed and I found someone who is going or coming ... I wasn't sure which!"

———>•<———

Grandma remarked that the only time overweight makes you feel better is when you see it on someone you might have married.

———>•<———

An elderly woman wandered out into the street after a cop had tried to wave her back to the curb. "Lady!" the cop roared, "Don't you know what it means when I hold up my hand?"

"I sure as heck ought to, officer," she replied. "I've been a school teacher for thirty-five years."

———>•<———

Hollywood is where, if a fellow's wife looks like a new woman, she probably is.

———>•<———

After Christmas, a woman remarked to her friend: "I came into contact this Christmas with a happy, bearded guy with a bag over his shoulder full of dirty laundry ... it was my son home from college with his laundry."

———>•<———

Q: What do you call a guy who never goes to church?
A: A Seventh Day Absentist.

"Yes, Krause, I'd quit this job in a sec if it wasn't for the prestige, power and money."

America still has more marriages than divorces and that just goes to prove that preachers sure can out-talk lawyers.

He: "Darling, here is your engagement ring."
She: "But this stone has a flaw in it."
He: "Forget that. Love is blind, and we're in love."
She: "But I'm not stone blind."

Mother calling to her daughter: "Dream boat ... your barnacle is here."

———⟫●⟪———

The grief-stricken woman threw herself across the grave and cried: "Oh, my God, how senseless life is! I'm no good without you. If only you hadn't died, how different this world would have been."

A clergyman happened to pass by, saw the grieving woman and said, "Brace yourself, my dear, all of us suffer like that at one time or another. I assume that was someone of deep importance to you?"

"Important? You bet it was. She was my husband's first wife."

———⟫●⟪———

Girl #1: "Didn't it make you ecstatically nervous when your boyfriend gave you all those lovely gifts?"
Girl #2: "Nope. I just stayed calm and collected."

———⟫●⟪———

Did you know that high heels was an invention of a girl who had been kissed on the forehead too many times?

———⟫●⟪———

The cop ran up to the man who'd been hit by a motorist and asked, "Did you get the number?"

"No, officer, I didn't. But I know who did it. I could recognize my wife's laughter anywhere."

———⟫●⟪———

At a commuter train station, a policeman noticed a woman huddled over her steering wheel. He went up to her saying, "Can I help you ma'am?"

She answered: "For ten years I have been driving my husband to this station to catch the train to work, but this morning I forgot him."

"She's my wife. These days it takes two incomes to get by."

The old lady was in the hospital recovering from a serious operation. It was her birthday and she'd gotten no card or presents from her family.

A day after the operation, her four sons came to visit her and brought nothing. After a brief conversation with her sons, the lady said, "Well, I see that once again you forgot your mother's birthday!"

The sons were very apologetic and said they had been so busy they'd forgotten.

"Don't worry about it," the old lady said. "I forgive you. You inherited forgetfulness from me. Gosh, I even forgot to marry your father."

"What! That means that we are all ..."

"That's right!" said the old lady. "And cheap ones at that!"

―――――

She Was Only a ...

Introduction

The human category of "She Was Only a ..." has disappeared but should not have. Here are some old-timers that are still cute:

- She was only a creditor's daughter, but she allowed no *advances*.
- She was only a grave-digger's daughter, but you ought to see her lower the *beer*.
- She was the village *belle*, so I gave her a *ring*.
- She was only a fireman's daughter, but she sure did like to go *blazes*...
- She was only a milkman's daughter, but she was the *cream* of the crop.
- She was only a photographer's daughter, but she was well *developed* ...
- She was only a plumber's daughter, but oh, those *fixtures* ...
- She was only a blacksmith's daughter, but she knew how to *forge ahead*.
- She was only a golfer's daughter, but her *form* was perfect ...
- She was only a lumberman's daughter, but she had been through the *mill*.
- She was only a carpenter's daughter, but she *nailed* her man ...

- She was only a teacher's daughter, but she was the college *pet.*
- She was only the stage manager's daughter, but she had the loveliest *props* ...
- She was only an optician's daughter. Two glasses and she made a *spectacle* of herself.
- She was only a taxidermist's daughter, and, boy, she knew her *stuff* ...
- She was only a watch-maker's daughter, but she gave me a wonderful *time.*

> Quoted from *The Pelican*
> University of California Press
> 1960

Wife: "Dear, I must tell you that I talked with the aerobics instructor this morning and he told me to come to class wearing loose clothes."
Husband: "Good idea. What did you say to that?"
Wife: "I told him if I had any loose clothing, I wouldn't need an aerobics class!"

I am free of all prejudice. I hate everyone equally.
> W.C. Fields

A Hollywood actress was suffering from nervous exhaustion and strain. She visited her psychiatrist who told her she needed to change her daily routine. "You need a change," he announced.

"A change! Let me tell you that in the past eight years I have been in six different plays, have lived in eight different apartments, have married three guys, have had six cats and have been to 13 states and six countries. What kind of change did you have in mind?"

"Aren't you supposed to say something sweet and welcoming when I come home from work, instead of 'oh, it's YOU again'?"

I'd like to be reborn as an oyster. Then I'd have to be good only from September until April.

Gracie Allen

Charlie Kelly was on his death bed when his wife tiptoed in and asked if he had any last requests.

"Yes, dear, I do. I'd love to have a big piece of that great chocolate cake you just baked. OK?"

"Oh, I'm sorry dear, that's for the wake."

———>⊃●⊂<———

Mother Superior: "Sister Mary, if you were walking through town and a man accosted you, what would you do?"

Sister Mary: "I would lift my habit, Mother Superior."

Mother Superior: "And what would you do next?"

Sister Mary: "I would tell him to drop his pants."

Mother Superior, now quite shocked: "And then what?"

Sister Mary: "I would run away. I can run much faster with my habit up than he can run with his pants down."

———>⊃●⊂<———

Typical male joke: "What's the advantage in having a woman as President of the United States?"

"We wouldn't have to pay her as much."

———>⊃●⊂<———

Q: Why are men happy?

A: Because ignorance is bliss.

———>⊃●⊂<———

A woman owned a store and was shocked to learn that next to her a new store, similar to her own, would soon open. They had erected a sign that read "THE BEST DEALS."

But things got worse ... Another store opened on the other side of hers and put up a huge sign that read:

"LOWEST PRICES" ... She was desolate until she got a great idea. She put a sign over her door reading: "ENTRY HERE."

———➤●◄———

"I wouldn't worry so much about your son playing with dolls," the psychiatrist told his patient's mother.

The mother replied: "I'm not, but his wife is terribly worried."

———➤●◄———

"My toughest fight was with my first wife."

Muhammad Ali

———➤●◄———

A guy is going into a doctor's office when he sees a nun running out, screaming wildly.

The guy walks into the office and says to the doctor: "Hey, Doc, what goes with the nun?"

The doctor relied: "Oh, I just told her she was pregnant."

The guy says, shocked: "You told her she was pregnant?"

The doctor relied, "Yes, and it sure did cure her hiccups!"

———➤●◄———

A man, despite some similarities — is not like dog droppings. For one thing, he's probably too big to just step over.

Dorion Yeager

———➤●◄———

A certain executive and his wife have a joint checking account. When he calls to say he'll be working late, if he doesn't get home by midnight, she starts checking the joints.

Man — the only animal that plays poker.

Don Herold

—————>●<—————

A woman sent this letter to the Internal Revenue Service: "Two years ago I deliberately falsified my tax return, and my conscience has not quit bothering me ever since. Please put the enclosed $75 on my account and if I still can't sleep at night, I'll send the other $600!"

—————>●<—————

A man's home may seem to be his castle on the outside; inside is more often his nursery.

Claire Booth Luce (1903-1987)

—————>●<—————

The telephone rang and Bill picked it up to hear a male voice say: "Bill, our monthly poker game is tonight. Can I pick you up?"

"Nope. I can't go tonight. Something has come down here at home," Bill said.

"Come down? I think you mean come up, don't you, Bill?" asked his friend.

"Nope, I mean come down. It's my wife's foot!"

—————>●<—————

The only time a woman succeeds in really changing a man is when he is a baby.

Natalie Wood (1938-1981)

—————>●<—————

An aggressive insurance salesman made a call on a young woman just after she'd been married, saying, "Now that you're married, I'm sure you'll want to take out more insurance."

"Sorry," she replied, "but I know him real well and he isn't that dangerous."

Women like silent men. They think they're listening.

> Marcel Achard in Quote
> November 4, 1956

Shortly after their marriage, the man died and the poor lady complained that he'd left her no insurance, "not a dime did he leave me."

"That's odd," replied her friend, "I heard he left you the money to buy that huge diamond in the ring you are wearing."

"Not really. It was part of his burial policy. He left $5,000 for the casket and fifteen thousand for the stone. This is the stone."

The broker called Mrs. Jones, an old client of his who was over seventy years of age. "I have really good news for you, Mrs. Jones," the broker said. "You won 1000 shares of Sears Roebuck and they've split."

"I'm sorry to hear that, sir," she replied. "Why, they've been together for over fifty years."

If man is little lower than the angels, the angels should reform.

> Mary Wilson Little

There was a shortage of steel in World War I. Then, some ladies donated their corsets. They had enough steel to build two battleships, from the steel supports in the corsets.

At a recent Arabian dance the performers all danced sheik-to-sheik.

—————

Did you hear about the oft-divorced movie star who, when mourning her fifth husband, asked to have black olives in her martinis.

It was the small town's only restaurant and the woman guest had ordered coffee. She took a taste and then said to the waitress, "This coffee is awful. What kind is it?"

"It's blended," the waitress replied.

"Blended?" was the response. "What kind of blend?"

"Last week and this week's coffee," was the answer.

A woman was talking with her friend and said: "I don't know what to do about my son. He has been away at college for two years and he hasn't learned to drink or shoot craps."

"Gee, you sure are lucky. Why in the world would you want him to learn to drink and play with dice?"

"Because," said the first woman, "he drinks and shoots craps."

———>•<———

A committee is a group of women who talk about a problem when they should be working at it.

———>•<———

When the woman answered the phone a voice asked: "When are you coming over? We've been waiting at Sally's house for an hour."

Thinking the call might be for one of her teenagers, she asked: "To whom did you wish to speak?"

"Sorry," the voice said, "I'm certain I've got the wrong number. Nobody I know ever says 'whom'."

———>•<———

The newly elected U.S. Senator was having her first press conference. A reporter from the newspaper that had opposed her, tried to embarrass her with this question: "Senator, when you get to Washington, will you give in to the powerful forces that everyone knows control you?"

The Senator replied: "I would appreciate it if you would confine your questions strictly pertaining to my congressional office and not to my husband!"

———>•<———

The first formula for lipstick was reddy in 1908.

When thread was first invented, everybody said, "Darn it!"

———>●<———

The woman chairperson at a United Givers fund raising dinner said to the orchestra leader: "As I come to the end of my speech tonight, I am going to call on everyone in the audience who will pledge $1000 to stand up. As exactly that moment I want your orchestra to play some appropriate music."

"And what music would you consider appropriate?" the conductor asked.

"Why the *Star Spangled Banner*, of course!"

———>●<———

The inventor of surgical stitches wrote on her first display box: "Suture self."

———>●<———

The mutual fund salesman was trying to sell old Mrs. Fox some of his mutual funds. He called her for an appointment and she said: "Come this evening if you wish. But, I am not sure if I want to invest in mutual funds. I already own some bonds and some industrials. So, Sir, if you come this evening, you'll find me in a dilemma."

"Oh, don't let that worry you, Ma'am," the salesman said, "The lady I called on last night was wearing a kimono."

———>●<———

In 1933 the French paid their debt to the US by shipping us five million hot dogs in payment of their debt to us of five million franks.

———>●<———

A lady stopped in a jewelry store to get a ring appraised. "My boyfriend gave it to me and I'm embarrassed to tell you I don't know how to pronounce the name of the stone. It is turkoise or turkwhoise?"

The jeweler studied it a bit, then said that the right way to pronounce the name was "glass."

———⋙⊙⋘———

The inventor of the reclining chair himself got a chair of profits from the manufacturer.

———⋙⊙⋘———

The wife had her husband in court for beating her. The judge asked her attorney: "Sir, the charge against her husband says that he beat her with an oak leaf. Now how could anybody hurt anyone beating them with so fragile an item as an oak leaf?"

"I understand your concern, your honor, but just let me tell you," the woman's attorney said, "that it was from their dining room table."

"I tried buying him tasteful clothes, but his body keeps rejecting them."

Did you know that knitted sox were first used as hand warmers, but later went down to defeat.

You don't have to be a careful weeder to own lawn care books.

The third grade teacher was getting to know her pupils on the first day of school...she turned to one little girl and asked: "What does your Daddy do?"

The little girl replied: "Whatever my Mom tells him to do."

Some bright guy invented the skateboard in 1962 and it was a wheely great idea.

When they first canned chicken broth Americans all thought it was souper.

The trial lawyer was examining a little old lady who had witnessed the serious auto accident.

"Tell the jury, Ma'am, if it is true, as we think, that the driver made only a cursory examination of the damaged car after the accident?"

"That's right, sir," said the old lady. "In fact, it was so derned cursory that it embarrassed me and everybody else who heard him. I had to plug my ears to keep from hearing the dad-blamed man curse!"

The first pantsuits for ladies were ready in 1965 but lots of ladies tried to skirt the issue.

————>>●<<————

In 1914 pancake makeup was issued to the public. But most women still preferred syrup.

————>>●<<————

The repairman got out of his truck and walked to the door where it was opened by the lady of the house. "Madam, you called for us to come out here for a repair to something in your house that doesn't work."

"Come right in, Sir," the lady said. "You'll find him on the couch."

————>>●<<————

Men couldn't use hair rollers when first invented because they were only for curls.

————>>●<<————

The first ship's dock was built by a guy who was revered by his pier group.

————>>●<<————

Grandma said to the little four-year-old. "Your mother tells me that you've been a very good little girl this past month, and for that I'm going to give you a bright, shiny penny."

"Grandma, if you don't mind," said the little girl, "I would rather have a dirty, muddy dime."

————>>●<<————

The first thing Betsy Ross did after she invented the flag was to ask visitors their opinion of it. That was America's first flag-poll.

"Marry me, Gracie. We still have a year or two left to kick up our heels."

It was a big let-down when high heels went out of style.

The newspaper reporter was interviewing the town's oldest citizen, a 101-year-old lady. "Tell our readers, dear lady," the reporter began, "whether or not you've lived in this county all your life."

"Not yet," she replied.

There's a wonderful leather woman's belt now on sale that costs only 98 cents. Less than a buckle.

In 1598 the first-ever twins were born on a two's-day.

===>●<===

Q: What has ten legs and an IQ of fifty?
A: Five guys watching a football game.

===>●<===

Sally described her seafood salad as shrimply awful.

===>●<===

Only a few years ago, the French sculptress created a statue of one of their most famous generals. It was known as DeGaulle stone.

===>●<===

The first wigs came to this country from China...and by hair mail, at that!

===>●<===

Man...a rational animal who always loses his temper when he is called upon in accordance with the dictates of reason.

Oscar Wilde, 1900

===>●<===

The guy was walking down the road when he saw a sign that said, "Bear Left." He got real scared and went home.

===>●<===

This same guy once stayed up all night studying for a urine test.

Did you hear about the dumb guy who planted Cheerios in his backyard hoping for a doughnut crop?

————>⊃●⊂————

The bachelor is a peacock, the engaged man a lion, and the married man a jackass...

German proverb

————>⊃●⊂————

Paul wasn't too bright. He saw a notice in the post office: "MAN WANTED FOR ROBBERY IN TEXAS." He read the sign, then said, "Too bad that job isn't in Iowa, or I'd take it."

————>⊃●⊂————

Maleness is wonderful, really, isn't it, honey? Perfect denial of all reality.

Erica Jong,
Any Woman's Blues, 1990

————>⊃●⊂————

Tim was bragging about his son. "He's so smart he can spell his name forward or backward," he bragged.
"What's his name?"
"Bob."

————>⊃●⊂————

Much male fear of feminism is infantilism — the longing to recover; thy mother's son, to possess a woman who exists purely for him. These infantile needs of adult men for women have become sentimentalized and romanticized enough as "love;" it is time to recognize them as arrested development.

Adrienne Rich

Q: How many men does it take to pop popcorn?
A: Three. One to hold the pan, and two others to show off by shaking the stove.

—————◦————

A Kansas man met his son's school teacher in the supermarket. "I hate to tell you this, sir," said the teacher, "but your boy is illiterate."

"That's a damned lie," the father shouted, "His mom and me was married almost a year before he was borned."

—————◦————

A gentleman once asked: "Why do women so utterly lack a sense of humor?"

Answer: God did it on purpose, so that we may love you men instead of laugh at you.

Mrs. Patrick Campbell, c. 1910

—————◦————

When God created man, she was only joking.

Anonymous

—————◦————

If men knew what women laughed about, they would never sleep with us.

Erica Jong

—————◦————

If the world were a logical place, men would ride side saddle.

Rita Mae Brown
Sudden Death, 1983

Q: What has an IQ of seven?
A: Eight men.

———————

Did you hear about the guy who went to the dentist complaining that his gums were shriveling and his teeth were falling out?

The dentist examined his teeth, then asked, "Do you brush your teeth? Your mouth is so bad that I doubt it."

"But I shore do brush 'em," said the guy.

"What do you brush them with?" asked the dentist.

"Preparation H," was the reply.

Q: What did God say after creating man?
A: I can do better.

Offer two reasons why men don't mind their own business:
1. No mind.
2. No business.

———————

A married couple was having a big fight at breakfast. "I never would have believed it possible for one woman to be so beautiful and so stupid," said the husband.

"It's merely God's will," she answered. "He made me beautiful so I'd be attractive to you. He made me stupid so you'd be attractive to me."

———————

Q: What can't a man keep? A job, a promise, a budget?
A: All three of the above.

———————

The Thompsons were taking their first train ride ever, A short time after the train started, the wife said to her husband, "The conductor told me that soon we'll be going under a river."

"Well," said hubby, "don't just sit there. Close the windows!"

———————

Q: How come is it that a man has a clean conscience?
A: Because he never uses it.

———————

Tanya and Emil had a really bad argument. So that night Emil decided to make up so he fixed supper. He did that and served it. Almost at once his wife said, "This steak tastes terrible."

"I know it," he said. "I burnt it just a little, but I put suntan oil on it so that it wouldn't taste bad."

Ducking for apples. Change one letter and it's the story of my life.

Dorothy Parker

—————————

Never go to a doctor whose office plants have died.

Erma Bombeck

—————————

A woman supplier of equipment to the state wanted to curry favor with an important (to her) manager. She offered to give him a new automobile. "Madam, the ethics of my office forbid me to take such a gift," the employee of the state replied.

"I can understand your feelings," said the woman, "but suppose instead of giving it to you I sell it to you for $35.00. Would that allow you to take it?

The guy replied: "Madam with such an offer as that, I'll take two of them."

"At least he's normal; well, as normal as men get."

Did you hear about the Oklahoma farmer who took his pregnant wife to the super store because he heard they had free delivery?

—————><•<—————

Love conquers all things except poverty and toothaches.

Mae West

—————><•<—————

A woman had reached her hundredth birthday and a friend asked her: "I know you don't drive or go to the cinema but are there other disadvantages to being 100 years old?"

"Only one thing I can think of just now," she replied. "It upsets me to see my grandkids reaching middle age."

—————><•<—————

If you think nobody cares if you are alive or dead, try missing a couple of car payments.

Ann Landers

—————><•<—————

A woman walked into a government relief office and asked: "Is this the main office of the war on poverty?"

"It is," the head of the office replied.

"I have come to surrender," the woman said.

—————><•<—————

From birth to age eighteen, a girl needs good parents. From eighteen to thirty-five she needs good looks. From thirty-five to fifty-five she needs a good personality. And from fifty-five on she needs cash.

Sophie Tucker

I think, therefore, I'm single.

> Lizz Winstead

———————

Husband: "Dearie, don't you think our son gets his brains from me?"
Wife: "I suppose so, dear. I still have all of mine."

———————

They say that a woman's dress should be tight enough to show that there's a woman inside and loose enough to show that she is a lady.

———————

A guy and his wife were driving home from a cocktail party when she said to him: "Honey, you made an absolute fool out of yourself this evening. I sure do hope that nobody realized you were sober."

———————

Grass widow on why she wants only female pallbearers: If those ol' boys won't take me when I'm alive, I shore don't want 'em taking me out when I'm dead.

———————

(Suggested epitaph for herself) Excuse my dust.

> Dorothy Parker

———————

While at dinner, the son, Herbie, said to his Dad: "I had a lot of trouble at school today, Dad, and it's all your fault."
"Why is that?" Dad responded.
"Well, Dad, remember last night at dinner I asked you how much $600,000 was?"

"Yes, I remember."
"Well, 'One heluva lot' isn't the right answer."

<hr />

"I'm so proud of Jennifer, my daughter," said Father. "She's taking both algebra and French. Please, Jenny, say something in algebra for us."

<hr />

A young lady announced her engagement to an older man. He was worth lots of money but his neighbors thought him eccentric and strange.

One of the girl's friends asked her: "Why would you want to marry that oddball? Everybody knows he's half-cracked."

"Maybe so," replied the girl, "But he sure isn't broke."

<hr />

> Papa loved Mamma,
> Mamma loved men
> Mamma's in the graveyard
> Papa's in the pen.
>
> Carl Sandburg

<hr />

There is nothing more demoralizing than a small but adequate income.

Edmund Wilson

<hr />

Diplomacy is the art of saying, "Nice man, nice man," until you locate a rolling pin.

<hr />

The husband was arrogant, stubborn and hardheaded.

The wife said to him: "You always think you're right. And you know good and well that you're wrong!"

"I agree. There has been a time when I was wrong. It was one time when I thought I was wrong and wasn't."

———>●<———

If I were married to her, I'd be sure to have dinner ready when she got home.

> George Schultz about Margaret Thatcher

———>●<———

Literature is mostly about having sex and not much about having children; life is the other way around.

———>●<———

I grew up with six brothers. That's how I learned to dance...waiting for the bathroom.

> Bob Hope

———>●<———

The woman was telling her friend: "My son has a Ph.D., my daughter has an A.B., and her hubby has an M.A. My nephew has a B.S. But my husband is the only one in the family with a J.O.B."

———>●<———

A smart alec guy stepped on the elevator of a New York skyscraper and tried to impress the elevator operator, saying, "I bet you have your ups and downs. Don't all these stops and starts wear you out?"

"Oh," she said, "I don't mind the starts and stops, it's just the 'jerks' that get me down!"

———>●<———

I used to be Snow White but I drifted.

> Mae West

157

Most women hate limericks, for the same reason calves hate cookbooks.

Gershon Legman

———>●<———

"My husband just installed an item that our grandkids are gonna get a big bang out of."

"What did he do?" her friend asked.

"He installed a screen door," was her reply.

———>●<———

Contraceptives: What Protestants use on all conceivable occasions.

Anonymous

———>●<———

Don't get annoyed if your neighbor plays his Hi-fi at two o'clock in the morning. Call him at four o'clock and tell him how much you enjoyed it.

———>●<———

A woman sued for divorce on the grounds that her husband was an alcoholic.

"This is quite strange," said the judge. "Didn't you know before you married him that he was a heavy drinker? Please explain this matter."

"No, your Honor, I did not know he was an alcoholic. I didn't discover that until one night when he came home sober."

———>●<———

Doctor Louise: "You should take a warm bath every evening before retiring."

Patient Dan: "How will that help me? I don't retire for thirty years."

Pas de deux: father of twins
Coup de grace: lawnmower

All men are of the same mould. But, some are mouldier than others.

Could it be that the wicked do well in this world while saints do well in the next?

The doctor was concluding his examination of the woman and noticed that her shins were bruised, scared and raw.

"What do you play?" the doctor asked; "Hockey, soccer or lacrosse?"

"Not any of them," the patient replied. "The only game I play is bridge."

Mary Glaze was as good as her word; she went to the tax office to pay her taxes with a smile, but they wouldn't accept that. They wanted cash.

John and Susie are happily married. They live in an apartment overlooking the rent.

CARPENTER...

"Say something! I want to make sure you're my child
before I give you a bath."

CHAPTER FIVE

**Many women will laugh at the drop of a hat,
especially if the man is still in it.**

A little 84-year-old woman got off the bus late one night
and headed for the senior center a few blocks away. Half
way there, a robber pulled her to one side and demanded
her money.

This 84-year-old gal was pretty level-headed and
shrewd. She said to the robber: "Young man, you should be
ashamed of yourself robbing an old woman like me.
Where's your ambition? You should be out robbing one of
those all-night convenience stores, not a little old lady like
me."

—————

Maybelle loves to go to church. She says she's learned that
faith will move mountains...but not furniture.

—————

An after-dinner speech ought to be like a lady's dress: long
enough to cover the subject but short enough to be
interesting.

—————

"How come is it that you are dating a guy who is forty
years older than you?" a woman asked her friend.

"Because we like each other's company," was the reply.
"He tells me he likes mine and I sure do like his...he calls it
the First National Bank."

I always keep a supply of whiskey in case I see a snake. And I always keep one on hand.

> W. C. Fields

He that looketh at a plate of ham and eggs and lusts after it, hath already committed breakfast within his heart.

> C. S. Lewis

During the summer, a young woman and man fell in love and he asked her to marry him. When he told her he had only $3,000 in the bank, she said that wouldn't do. She wouldn't marry him until he had $10,000 in the bank.

That ended the discussion of marriage and money until Christmas came around; the young man told her he'd been able to save only a total of $5,000.

"Well, George," she told him, "things are kind of tough now so that's close enough. I'll marry you."

I don't care what is written about me so long as it isn't true.

> Dorothy Parker

My husband is German. Last night I dressed up as Poland and he invaded me.

> Bette Midler

There is so little difference between husbands, you might as well keep the first.

> Adela Rogers St. John

My husband is living proof that women can take a joke.

> Sheila Myers Bumpe Stioker

When the cute girl of 25 told her friends that she was going to marry a 66-year-old guy, her friends were horrified.

"Dear, you know these May and December marriages don't work out. Everybody knows what December finds in you...youth, beauty, charm, the very breath of spring...but what will May find in December?"

"Santa Claus," was her reply.

———⟫●⟪———

If they can put one man on the moon, why can't they put them all there?

Unknown

———⟫●⟪———

Much admired actress Mrs. Patrick Campbell called marriage "the deep, deep peace of the double bed after the hurly-burly of the chaise lounge."

———⟫●⟪———

A woman visited a psychiatrist for the first time. He invited her to sit back on the couch and make herself comfortable. He saw that she hesitated and said, "Please, do sit back on the couch. I ask all my patients to do just that."

The woman did as instructed and smoothed out her dress over her knees.

"Now," the doctor said, "Let's begin. First off, tell me...how did your troubles begin?"

"Exactly like this," was her reply.

———⟫●⟪———

A woman's guess is much more accurate than a man's certainty.

Rudyard Kipling
Three and an Extra
Plain Tales from the Hills, 1888

Women want mediocre men, and men are working hard to be as mediocre as possible.

> Margaret Mead
> *Quote*, May 15, 1958

—————>⊛<—————

"How is it that you don't play golf with Peter anymore?" the wife asked her husband.

"I'm sure you wouldn't play with a guy who cheats all the time, would you?" her husband asked.

"Certainly not!" she replied.

"Well, neither will Peter."

—————>⊛<—————

Whatever women do, they must do twice as well as men to be thought half as good. Luckily, that is not difficult.

> Charlotte Whitton, on becoming
> mayor of Ottawa, Ontario, 1963

—————>⊛<—————

Never go to bed mad. Stay up and fight.

> Phyllis Diller's *Housekeeping Hints*

—————>⊛<—————

Safety for women? Try removing men.

> Ellen Goodman, *News-Press*, 1990

—————>⊛<—————

Mothers are a biological necessity; fathers a social invention.

> Margaret Mead

—————>⊛<—————

Two guys with their wives were having dinner one night when one of the guys observed: "There must be some place where the salary is great, but someone else does the work, and gets all the blame when things go wrong."

One of the wives said, "Just ask me. I'm a secretary. Any secretary knows the answer. Just ask any secretary about her boss!"

⋙⋘

The vote, I thought, means nothing to women. We should be armed.

Edna O'Brien

"Can you come back next week and demonstrate it yet again?"

A woman from the city was visiting her cousin on a farm in Illinois. The guy had to go to town but left instructions with his city cousin as to what she should do when the guy from Semato came to artificially inseminate one of his cows.

"I've left a nail by the stall of the cow I want inseminated," he told his cousin and then left.

The inseminator arrived at the farm that afternoon and the girl took him to the barn and to the stall with the nail.

"What's the nail for?" asked the inseminator.

Sally thought for a moment, then said, "I guess for hanging up your pants!"

DICKSON'S JOKE TREASURY

Knock, Knock
Who's there?
Flo.
Flo who?
Flo ride is good for your teeth.

Knock, Knock
Who's there?
Henrietta and Juliet.
Henrietta and Juliet who?
Henrietta big dinner and got sick; Juliet the same thing but she's okay.

Knock, Knock
Who's there?
Isabel.
Isabel who?
Isabel necessary on a bicycle?

Knock, Knock
Who's there?
Just Diane.
Just Diane who?
Just diane to meet you.

Knock, Knock
Who's there?
Marion.
Marion who?
Marion in haste, repent at leisure.

Knock, Knock
Who's there?
Mandy.
Mandy who?
Mandy lifeboats.

Knock, Knock
Who's there?
Polly Warner.
Polly Warner who?
Polly warner cracker?

Knock, Knock
Who's there?
Sarah.
Sarah who?
Sarah doctor in the house?

Knock, Knock
Who's there?
Thelma.
Thelma who?
Thelma, pretty maiden, are there any more at home like
you?

Knock, Knock
Who's there?
Vera.
Vera who?
Vera interesting.

Knock, Knock
Who's there?
Winnie.
Winnie who?
Winnie you going to print better jokes?

Knock, Knock
Who's there?
Yvonne.
Yvonne who?
Yvonne to be alone?

Knock, Knock
Who's there?
Barcelona.
Barcelona who?
My sister, she doesn't go into bars alone.

Knock, Knock
Who's there?
Butch, Jimmy and Joe.
What about Butch, Jimmy and Joe?
Butch your arms around me, Jimmy a kiss, or I'll Joe home.

Knock, Knock
Who's there?
Celeste.
Celeste who?
Celeste time I'll call you.

Knock, Knock
Who's there?
Delores.
Delores who?
Delores be an England.

Knock, Knock
Who's there?
Cirrhosis.
Cirrhosis who?
Cirrhosis red, violets are blue.

Knock, Knock
Who's there?
Thistle.
Thistle who?
Thistle be the last knock knock joke.

Why did the fish want to make love?
She had a haddock.

                                 × × × × × × × × × × × × × × × ×

Why did the crustacean divorce her husband?
He was an old crab.

                                 × × × × × × × × × × × ×

"Mom, there was a guy here today to see you."
"Did he have a bill?"
"Nope, just a nose like yours."

                                 × × × × × × × × × × × ×

    "I had a great vacation in California," the woman told the man seated next to her in the plane taking her home.
    "That's good to hear," replied the man, "Where did you stay?"
    "In San Jose," was her reply.
    "Lady, in California we pronounce the J, like H. We say San Hosay. How long did you stay?"
    "About two months, all of Hune and Huly."

                                   × × × × × × × × × × × ×

    The woman violinist was having a concert and, at intermission, came on stage and announced to the audience: "This violin I'm playing was made in 1778."
    A voice from the audience asked: "Was it a personal gift to you then?"

                                   × × × × × × × × × × × ×

    Maria Elena was a successful business executive. She called her staff together and announced, "I'm going to make a salary increase."
    "Great," one male employee said. "When does it become effective?"
    "When you do!" was the reply.

                                   × × × × × × × × × × × ×

    The business executive was sitting beside a woman minister during a long and stormy trip to Chicago. The man was getting very upset at the violent storm outside, shaking the plane and lighting the plane with lightening. "Madam Minister," said the executive, "You are a lady of God. Can't you do something, pray for something that'll end this terrible storm?"

The lady replied, "Sorry, sir, I'm in sales, not management."

The office manager is ordered into the president's office and the boss says to her: "Sally, there's $75,000 missing from the safe and you and I are the only ones who know the combination. Would you explain yourself?"

"Sir, let's each of us chip in $37,500 and forget the entire matter."

What's the difference between a barber and a woman with many kids?

One has razors to shave and the other has shavers to raise.

> Paul Dickson
> *Dickson's Joke Treasury*
> Adapted by permission of John Wiley
> & Sons, 1984, 1992

Two women, both business executives, met outside the door of a psychiatrist and one asked the other..."Are you coming or going?"

The one who was asked replied: "If I knew that I wouldn't be here."

Two old friends met at the supermarket and began to reminisce...

"So, tell me, Gracie, how is your son, Emil, doing?"

"He's doing fine. He's a poet and just got his Master's degree from the University of Illinois."

"And what about Janie?"

"She's doing great, too. She graduated last year with a degree in Modern Art."

"Wonderful. And how is my favorite, Georgie, doing?"

"Georgie is a plumber. He refused to go to college. He loves to work with his hands. He's now a plumber. And if it weren't for Georgie, we'd all be starving!"

Verily, men do foolish things thoughtlessly, knowing not why. But a woman doeth aught without a reason.

> Gelett Burgess
> *The Maxims of Methuslah*, 1907

Man is like a phonograph with half-a-dozen records. You soon get tired of them all: yet you have to sit at a table while he reels them off to every visitor.

> George Bernard Shaw
> *Preface to Getting Married*, 1911

One of the things that politics has taught me is that men are not a reasoned or reasonable sex.

> Margaret Thatcher

There was, I think, never any reason to believe in any innate superiority of the male, except his superior muscle.

> Bertrand Russell
> "Ideas That Have Haunted Mankind"
> *Unpopular Essays*, 1950

We don't just need a new generation of leadership, we need a new gender of leadership.

Governor Bill Clinton
to the Women's Caucus of the
Democratic National Convention
July, 1992

"That ain't no reason, Helen — lots of women marry idiots!"

The salesman stood outside the door talking to the lady of the house. She was a bit hard-of-hearing.

"Good morning," he said, "I'm a salesman for Hoosier Woolen Mills and we have a special price on our woolen yarns that didn't measure up to our high standards. The colors ran and the yarns are a bit off color. Can I come in and show them to you?"

The woman hadn't understood him well and said, "I'm sorry, what did you say?"

The salesman replied: "Would you be interested in some off-color yarns?"

"Sounds like fun," she replied, "Come on in and we'll have a cup of coffee while you tell them to me."

You can think of maleness as a kind of birth defect.

> Dr. Stephen Wachtel
> Memorial Sloan-Kettering Cancer
> Center (and others)

———◆———

The beast in me's eager and fit for a brawl.
Just rile me a bit and she'll kick down the walls.
I'll bawl to you fiend that you've no balls at all.

> Chorus of women in
> Aristophanes
> *Lysistrata*, 411 B.C.

———◆———

Our teenage daughter just lost her boyfriend to what she said was a mere passing fanny.

———◆———

"Woman does not live by bed alone," says Maria Gonzales, insurance executive.

———◆———

Women are natural guerrillas. We nestle into the enemy's bed, avoiding open warfare, watching the options, playing the odds.

> Sally Kempton

———◆———

Can you imagine a world without men? No crime and lots of happy, fat women.

> Nicole Hollander
> *Sylvia*

———◆———

Two old-maid sisters were sitting in the parlor. One of them said, "I'm reading the newspaper and it tells of a woman who had four husbands and each of them died and she had all four of them cremated."

"That's life for you," the sister replied. "Here we sit without ever having husbands and that woman has husbands to burn!"

———————

Of all the nasty outcomes predicted for women's liberation...none was more alarming, from a feminist point of view, than the suggestion that women would eventually become just like men.

> Barbara Ehrenreich
> "The Real and Ever-Widening
> Gender Gap"
> *Esquire*, June 1994

———————

So many men...so little ammunition!

> *Feminist Slogans*, 1993

———————

Paul Edwards and his wife returned home from the theater and said to the babysitter: "I sure hope that little Peggy was as good as gold while we were gone."

"She was for over an hour..." the babysitter replied, "then she went off the gold standard."

———————

The thing to remember about fathers is, they're men.

> Phyllis McGinley
> Girl's Eye View of Relatives
> *Times Three*, 1960

———————

Cannon Father: Male who impregnates explosively and then exits the scene of the female's destruction; one anxious to replace himself without having to participate in his offspring's upbringing.

Women spend a tremendous amount of their income protecting themselves from unpleasant situations created by men...For the most part, women are a calming influence, peacefully beautifying the city...but men can squelch your appreciation for the outdoors by leering, honking, and making monkey-sucking noises if they find a woman attractive...Cut a woman a break. Cut us a deal in taxes.

> Lisa Nee
> Op-Ed page in the *New York Times*
> July 26, 1992

———————

My daughter shuns miniskirts so we call her hemlock.

———————

Fowl: A four-letter bird.

———————

Has it ever occurred to you that everybody who favors birth control has already been born?

———————

And now you are about to experience the ageless character of the conflict of women versus men. Some of these sayings and jokes go back 150 years so that all must realize that women placing men in an inferior status is not a new concept.

These remarks are multi-national — European and American — so that you will know that women of all nations have a very special way of relegating man to a certain inferior position, similar to the one that many American women today have chosen for themselves.

It is simply amazing the hateful, baneful ideas that some women offer about men. Some women seem to hate the very concept of maleness. And in what follows, you'll find examples of their outlook. Curiously, there are men included who mimic women in their exposition of the evilness of men.

By the time you swear you're his,
shivering and sighing,
And he vows his passion is
Infinite, undying,
Lady, make note of this:
One of you is lying.

Dorothy Parker, *Unfortunate Coincidence*, 1926
"One-liners"

My husband added some magic to our marriage: he disappeared.
Marriage is a romance in which the hero dies in the first chapter.
One of the surest signs that a woman is in love is when she divorces her husband.

Dolly Parton

Love is the quest; marriage the conquest; divorce the inquest.

Helen Rowland, *Reflections of a Bachelor Girl*, 1909

Marriage is a great institution, but I'm not ready for an institution.

                                        Mae West

I can't mate in captivity.

                    Gloria Steinem, on why she did not marry.

I'd rather be a free spirit and paddle my own canoe.

                        Louisa Mae Alcott, *Little Women*
                                                1868

I never married because I would have to give up my favorite hobby.

                                        Mae West

Women complain about sex more than men. Their gripes fall into two major categories: 1. Not enough and 2. Too much.

How do you feel about men? With my fingers.

                                            Cher

It's not the men in my life that count — it's the life in my men.

                                        Mae West

Had nature formed me of the other sex, I should certainly have been a rover.
                        Abagail Adams, April 20, 1771

The only reason I would take up jogging is so that I could hear heavy breathing again.

> Erma Bombeck

Why did God create man?
Because a vibrator can't mow the lawn.

Why is a man like a mortgage?
The interest is unwelcome and the demands never end.

Give a man a free hand and he'll run it all over you.

> Mae West 1892-1980

Give me charity and continence, but not yet.

> *Augustine, Confessions*, 5th century

People who are so dreadfully devoted to their wives are so apt, from mere habit, to get devoted to other people's wives as well.

> Jane Welsh Earlyle, on her faithless
> husband, c. 1860

Lady, Lady, should you meet
One whose ways are discreet,
One who murmurs that his wife
Is the lodestar of his life,
One who keeps assuring you
That he never was untrue,
Never loved another one...
Lady,' Lady, better run!

> Dorothy Parker
> *Social Note,* 1926

Trust not a man; we are by nature false,
Dissembling, subtle, cruel and inconstant.

Thomas Twnaav
The Orphan, 1680

No man worth having is true to his wife, or can be true to his wife, or ever was, or ever will be so.

Sir John Vanbrugh
The Relapse, 1607

What do you call a man with a third of a brain? Gifted.

Where do you find a man that is committed? In a mental hospital.

What do you call an intelligent man in America? A tourist.

What do you call a man who lost 80% of his brain? Newly divorced.

Why is a man like a laxative? They both irritate the crap out of you.

A man is incomplete until he is married. Then he is finished.

Zsa Zsa Gabor

A fool and his money are soon married.

Carolyn Wells

Diamonds are my service stripes.

Mae West

A girl must marry for love, and keep on marrying until she finds it.

Zsa Zsa Gabor

There are men I could spend eternity with. But not this life.

Kathleen Norris, *Blue Mountain*,
1980

Men are beasts, and even beasts don't behave as they do.

Brigitte Bardot

The more I see of men, the more I admire dogs.

Marie De Sevigne

Let us love dogs, let us only love dogs. Men and cats are unworthy creatures.

Maria Konstantiova Bashkirtsco
(1860-1884)

Some of my best leading men have been dogs and horses.

Elizabeth Taylor

I never married because there was no need. I have three pets at home which answer the same purpose as a husband. I have a dog which growls every morning, a parrot which swears all afternoon, and a cat that comes home late at night.

Marie Corelli (1855-1924)

Man is an animal that laughs and has a state legislature.

Samuel Butler (1835-1902)

Man is but little inferior to the tiger and the hyena in cruelty and savagery.

Samuel Butler

Man is the most formidable of all beasts of prey, and indeed, the only one that preys systematically on its own species.

William James (1842-1910)

The bachelor is a peacock, the engaged man a lion, and the married man a jackass.

German proverb

I have always thought that the difference between a man and a mule is that the mule can change his mind.

Abagail Dunway (1834-1915)

I like men to behave like men — strong and childish.

Francoise Sagan

A bachelor never quite gets over the idea that he is a thing of beauty and a boy forever.

Helen Rowland (1870-1950)

It is better for a girl to have beauty than brains because boys can see better than they think.

Man forgives woman anything except the wit to outwit him.

> Marie Antrim
> *Naked Truth* and *Veiled Illusions*
> 1922

A woman's appetite is twice that of man's; her sexual desires are four times; her intelligence is eight times.

I'm not denying that women are foolish: God made 'em to match the men.

> George Elliot
> *Adam Bede,* 1859

When he said we were trying to make a fool of him, I could only murmur that the creator had beat us to it.

> Helen Rowland
> c. 1925

A woman's advise is worthless, but he who does not take it is a fool.

> Spanish Proverb

I want to know why, if men rule the world, they don't stop wearing neckties.

> Linda Ellerbee
> Reprinted with permission
> *Move On,* 1991

"I wanted to get married and settle down, not get married and sink to the bottom!"

Give a man a fish and you feed him for a day. Teach a man
to fish and you get rid of him on the weekends.

Unknown

I want a man who is kind and understanding. Is that too
much to ask of a millionaire?

Zsa Zsa Gabor

A healthy male adult bore consumes each year one and a
half times his own weight in other people's patience.

John Updike
"Confessions of a Wild Bore"
in *Assorted Prose*
Alfred A. Knopf, 1965

Mountains appear more lofty the nearer they are approached, but great men resemble them not at all in this particular.

Marguerite Power
Countess of Bessomtom (1789-1849)

"War is menstrual envy."

Feminist antiwar slogan.

There are only two kinds of men — the dead and the deadly.

Helen Rowland

Scratch a lover, find a foe.

Dorothy Parker
Enough Rope, 1929

Macho does not prove mucho.

Zsa Zsa Gabor

"I am more and more convinced that man is a dangerous creature."

Abagail Adams to John Adams,
November 27, 1775

A little girl was watching her mother try on a fur coat and the little one said: "Mama do you know how many poor, dumb beasts had to suffer so you could have that coat?"
"Little girl, don't speak of your father like that."

(Sadie) gathered herself together. No-one could describe the scorn of her expression or the contemptuous hatred she put into her answer.

"You men! You filthy, dirty pigs! You're all the same, all of you. Pigs! Pigs!"

W. Somerset Maugham
Rain, 1923

——————

"Did you hear about the baby who was born bi-sexual?"
"What about him?"
"He was born with both a penis and a brain."

——————

Did you hear about the astringent-tongued lady who assured her friend: "Enjoy yourself while you can, after all, you only have nine lives."

——————

There would be a lot less divorce if husbands tried as hard to keep their wives as they did to get them.

——————

A woman politician was being interviewed on television on a variety of subjects, one of them was: "What do you think of birth control?"

"An interesting question," she replied. "Whenever I'm asked that question I remind myself that I have three brothers and six sisters older than myself."

——————

Bobby: "Dorothy doesn't seem to be very intelligent, does she?"
Jack: "No, she didn't pay any attention to me, either."

At breakfast, a guy said to his wife: "I know it's a miracle but this year I remember that next Wednesday will be your birthday. This is the first year I will have remembered. And you'll be 40 years old. What would you like for a present?"

"Not to be reminded of it," was her reply.

———⟫●⟪———

When a wife buys things on credit, she is only displaying confidence in her husband.

———⟫●⟪———

Behind every successful man there stands a woman, and the Internal Revenue Service...one to take the credit and the other to take the cash.

———⟫●⟪———

A guy goes into this famous French restaurant where the food was superb but the waiters spoke only French. The waiter brought him a chicken leg but the guy wanted white meat, so he called the waiter's attention to his hands, put them on his breast and nodded, then pointed at the leg and shook his head. The waiter nodded as if he understood, then returned with a glass of milk.

———⟫●⟪———

One pretty young girl to another: "It's just the little things about him that I like...he owns a small mansion, a small Cadillac and a small racing stable."

———⟫●⟪———

A lovely beauty queen who was a movie star, once applied for a visa. When she came to a blank that read: "single — married — divorced" — she wrote "everything."

"If people ask me what I see in you, Albert, what shall I tell them?"

———>●<———

"I've got the worst possible husband," the recent bride announced to her friend. His disposition is so nasty that I'm losing weight."

"If I were you I'd leave him," said her friend.

"I plan to do that," was the reply, "Only I'm waiting until he gets me down to 110 pounds."

———>●<———

Small girl showing bathroom scales to her young friend. "What's it for?" asked her friend.

"I don't really know," was the reply, "but when you stand on it, it makes you mad."

———>●<———

There is a minister in Chatham, Illinois who puts all his bills in a drawer marked: "Due unto others."

———>●<———

There is a sign outside a Chicago strip joint. It reads "Here the belles peel."

———>●<———

"What happened between Sally and George? They broke up, didn't they?"

"Yeah. It was a matter of religious beliefs, I think. He was broke and she worshiped money."

———>●<———

American Bra Association: a big holdup.

There was once an article in a financial journal about women having trouble getting credit. The article headline read: "No-Account-Females".

———>∞<———

J.B. Priestly put it just right. He said: "We should act toward our country as women act toward the men they love. A loving wife will do anything for her husband except stop criticizing and trying to improve him."

———>∞<———

One woman to another: "My husband is a boss spelled backward...you know: <u>double</u> S.O.B."

———>∞<———

At our Kiwanis picnic, we all had parts to play. I was dressed like a gypsy and told fortunes. A woman came in to get my services and I said to her: "I see a buried treasure."
The woman replied: "Oh, yes, I know all about that. It's my husband's first wife."

———>∞<———

A woman walked up to the teller in her bank and said: "I want to withdraw $50 from my husband's half of our joint account."

———>∞<———

A baby usually wakes up in the wee-wee hours of the morning.

———>∞<———

A naive woman phoned the airlines office and asked: "How long does it take to fly to New York?"
"Just a minute," the clerk replied.
"Thank you," the woman replied, and hung up.

"Wa'da ya mean 'ouch'?"

That same woman found her clothes line to be about two feet too long. So she called her husband and asked him to fix it. He moved the house two feet back!

———⪼●⪻———

Q: How do you drown a man?
A: Get him to push start a submarine.

Most everyone read in the papers about the guy, a terrorist, whose gang sent him to Chicago to blow up a bus, but he burnt his lips too badly on the exhaust pipe.

———⟫•⟪———

Q: How do you get a man to laugh at a joke on Monday?
A: Tell it to him on Friday.

———⟫•⟪———

"Hey," said the girl at the women's club meeting, "I've got some great jokes on men."
"Before you start, Sister, I must tell you I admire men."
"Don't worry, I'll tell the jokes slowly."

———⟫•⟪———

A doctor passed a nurse in the corridor. He cauterize and winked. She, interne, winked back.

———⟫•⟪———

The airplane was in trouble as it was coming in to Chicago.
"I've got real problems landing," the pilot called to the landing tower.
"It's okay to land," the tower called back. "Can you give us your height and position?"
"Well, sir, I'm five foot nine and sitting in the front of the plane," was the guy's reply.

———⟫•⟪———

Then there was the guy who, on his wedding night, sat up through the entire night, waiting for her sexual relations to arrive.

The poor girl was pregnant and sent her boyfriend to arrange for her to go to an abortion clinic. But he reported back to her that there was a twelve-month waiting list.

———————

Doctor: "Madam, your pulse is as steady as a clock."
Patient: "That's because you've got your finger on my wrist watch."

———————

The town was holding a male beauty contest but nobody won.

———————

An extremely nervous guy carried his twins up to the baptismal font to be christened.
　　"What are the names of the boy and girl?" asked the pastor.
　　"Steak and Kidney," was his reply.
　　"Pay no attention to him, pastor," said the wife. "Their names are Kate and Sidney."

———————

When you ask your husband to dig up the garden, the first thing he digs up is an excuse.

———————

　　The symphony treasurer warned the chairman of the fund-raising committee against asking for too much money of some attendees.
　　"Don't put all your begs in one askit."

"Holy smokes, Mother," the poet Whistler exclaimed as his mother mopped the floor, "Have you gone off your rocker?"

—————>●<—————

A father had spent the whole morning pouring a cement patio. He looked outside that afternoon to see his kids pressing their hands in the newly laid concrete. He opened the window and severely bawled-out the kids. His wife, upset by his words, said, "Don't you love your children?"

Hubby replied: "In the abstract, yes, I do, but not in the concrete!"

—————>●<—————

Looking up from the newspaper, the wife remarked to her husband: "It says here that some guy throttled his wife."

The husband replied: "Sounds like a practical choker."

—————>●<—————

Someone once asked Groucho Marx what he thought of women's rights.

In his usual way, he remarked, "I like both sides of them."

—————>●<—————

They tell this story about Martina Navratilova, the superb Czechoslovakian tennis star who defected to the United States. She repeatedly asked a State Department clerk: "Do you cache Czechs here?"

—————>●<—————

"I don't like neuritis," said the Springfield librarian. "Just offer me the old timers like Shakespeare, Maupin, Thackery and Dickens."

Sign in a reducing salon: "Stop, Wait and Lessen!"

——>●<——

Girls who don't repulse men's advances, advance men's pulses.

——>●<——

Nobody could pin anything on Lady Godiva.

——>●<——

The young couple were strolling through a pasture in the country. Paul got romantic and said to his sweetheart: "Nell, just look at that cow over there rubbing noses with her calf, isn't that sweet? I'd like to do the same thing."

"Well, go ahead. I don't think the cow would mind a bit."

——>●<——

A snowbound women's libber wrote of her yardman; "I sure was glad to see a male shovelist."

——>●<——

The bride said to her husband: "Let's get a new sports car. I'd like to hear the patter of a tiny Fiat."

——>●<——

"How about a ride with me, cutie pie?" the smart alec young fellow said to the girl as he rolled his car to a stop.

"Are you going North?" she asked.

"Sure am," he replied.

"Good," she replied, "give my regards to the Eskimos."

My husband added some magic to our marriage. He disappeared.

———————

First date: "I said, you must have been out with worse-looking guys than I , haven't you, Tillie?"
Tillie: "Be quiet. I heard you the first time. I'm trying to think."

———————

If it weren't for women, men would still be hanging from trees.

Zsa Zsa Gabor

———————

Rita: "Where's your brother, Mabel?"
Mabel: "He's in the hospital...his girlfriend threw him over."
Rita: "That's odd. How could that put him in the hospital?"
Mabel: "She threw him over a bridge."

———————

Wife to husband: "This Christmas, let's do things differently. Let's give one another sensible gifts, like ties and diamond rings."

———————

Tilly: "They tell me he's worth in the neighborhood of a million dollars."
Margaret: "Wonderful! That's my favorite neighborhood."

Absence makes the heart grow fonder in all categories except that of mothers-in-law.

———————

A woman went to a portrait artist and asked to have her picture painted. "But I want you to show me with more than the diamond ring I wear. I want you to show me with a pearl necklace, a diamond brooch, a gold and diamond encrusted bracelet and a pin loaded with rubies."

"I sure can do that, Ma'am. But may I ask why, if you don't own all that stuff, you want me to paint you with it?"

"Well, I'm getting a divorce and I'm going to send this painting to the bitch that is marrying my husband. When she sees all the jewelry he gave me, she'll make his life miserable till she gets the same thing!"

"My husband used to light up my life, but he came without batteries included."

"I hear you went to the doctor's office yesterday, Maizie. How did you make out?"

"OK, I guess. The doctor nearly found out what I had."

"What? What do you mean he nearly found out what you had?"

"That's correct. I had $40.00 and he charged me $35.00 for the call."

———⟶⊷⟵———

Man is the only animal to whom the torture and death of his fellow creatures is amusing in itself.

James A. Froude (1818-1894)

———⟶⊷⟵———

A rich businessman lost his wife but he fell in love with his secretary, who was much younger than he. He really gave his life to his new sweetheart, taking her out to dinner night after night, and to dances and shows after dinner. He was ready to ask her to marry him but he was an experienced businessman and had learned to be cautious. So he hired a detective to inquire after the young woman's past.

After several weeks, the agency reported to him that his girl had an absolutely clean past without scandal of any kind. "However," they reported, "Recently she has been seen repeatedly enjoying the nightlife of the city accompanied by an elderly man of questionable reputation."

———⟶⊷⟵———

Man — a creature made at the end of the week's work when God was tired.

Mark Twain

———⟶⊷⟵———

The woman had just returned from her college reunion and was talking of it to a friend.

"Was it fun?" the friend asked.

"Not really," was the reply. "All of my former classmates were so old and fat and wrinkled that none of them recognized me."

———⟫●⟪———

I sometimes think that God in creating man somewhat overestimated His ability.

Oscar Wilde (1854-1900)

———⟫●⟪———

Heaven save me from the smartest man in the world, at least when he is a conceited fool.

———⟫●⟪———

Two women were vacationing at a Miami Beach hotel and were on the beach. One said: "Just look at that gorgeous guy over there."

"Aw, he's not so much. Take away all those muscles, that cute, wavy hair, his broad chest and beautiful face and what have you got?"

"My husband," her friend replied.

———⟫●⟪———

He speaks to me as if I were a public meeting.

Queen Victoria (1819-1901)
on Gladstone

———⟫●⟪———

"Tell me Honey," said the husband to his wife, "Where does all that money I give you for food go?"

"If you'll just stand sideways in front of the mirrow, you'll know exactly where it goes."

———⟫●⟪———

The woman sat on the witness stand while being quizzed by the district attorney. "Mrs. Jason, would you tell the court

just why you shot your husband with a bow and arrow?"
Woman: "I didn't want to waken the children."

———————

A woman need know but one man to understand all men; whereas, a man may know all women and understand not one of them.

Helen Rowland

———————

Before Bob got married he used to say that he would be the boss or know the reason why. Now Bob's married and knows the reason why.

———————

There truly is such a thing as a happily married couple. It's any wife who's out with another woman's husband.

———————

Two women were talking about the deceased husband of a mutual friend. "He was really a good man," said one lady. "Very good to his family."

"He certainly was," the other replied. "He was so considerate...hardly ever home."

———————

Hari-Kari: Transporting a wig from one place to another.

———————

Two women were talking about the attributes of the ideal husband. One of the women said, "I want a guy who is musically inclined; can sing, dance, tell jokes and, most important, will stay home with me every night."

"Honey," said her friend, "I think you'd be better off with a TV set."

A lady pilot: a plane Jane.

———>●<———

College bred is a four-year loaf made from the old man's bread.

———>●<———

"I certainly did not marry my wife for her money," said the guy to his friend, "Just because she had a million dollars. Actually, I made her a millionaire."

"What was she before you married her?" his friend asked.

"A multi-millionaire," was his reply.

———>●<———

Mother to six-year-old son: "When you talk to visitors who come to see us, just say that I like to crochet. Don't tell them I'm the happy hooker."

———>●<———

The father was arguing with his wife over the wife's efforts to get their daughter married. "Don't be in such a hurry," the father shouted. "Let her wait till the right man comes along."

The mother replied: "I refuse to do that. I certainly didn't when I was her age."

———>●<———

A career girl's mind makes her go ahead, while a chorus girl makes her behind go.

"If you give my mom a raise, I'll not tell you that she called you a cheapskate."

CHAPTER SIX

The man who can laugh at himself never runs out of things he can laugh at.

"Mom, that hound dog is really vicious. I don't think you'll ever train him," her son said to his mom.

"Just you wait and see. You should have known your father when I married him."

———⟫●⟪———

Two women were chatting and discussing their children. "I have a hard time awakening my twelve-year-old every morning," said one.

Her friend replied, "You should use the system I use for my fourteen-year old."

"What is that?" asked her friend.

"I throw our cat on his bed to get him up."

"But how does that help?" the other asked.

"My kid sleeps with his dog," was the reply.

———⟫●⟪———

Laundress: A gown worn while sitting on the grass.

———⟫●⟪———

How to greet a girl named Katherine: "Lokate"

———⟫●⟪———

A husband and wife were having a terrible argument. At the top of their dispute, the husband yelled, "I wish I'd never married you. I should have taken my mother's advice."

"Are you trying to tell me that your mother told you not to marry me?"

"You got it right, Sis. She told me a hundred times I should stay away from you."

"Good golly," she moaned. "To think how I've misjudged that good woman all these years."

———>●<———

Minimum: A very small mother.

———>●<———

Protein: A favorable attitude towards teens.

———>●<———

Hubby was growing tired of all the hours he spent each month trying to balance his wife's bank statement. She worked every month to balance the account and then gave it to her husband to rectify.

One month she finished her work and said to her husband, "Finally! I balanced it. Here, please check it out for me."

And he did. He noticed a final entry marked ESP $72.00. "You did a good job, Honey. It balances fine. But what in the world is ESP?"

"Oh, that's just my entry for 'error some place'!"

———>●<———

Warehouse: What you say when you can't find your way home...

———>●<———

At Christmas, give your kids something that will separate the men from the toys.

Four guys broke into a residence of a famous modernistic painter. They tied her up, opened her wall safe and fled with $32,000 in cash. Friends stopped by the next day and released the woman.

She reported it to the police and when they came they asked: "Could you identify the robbers?"

"Sure. Easy. I'll draw you pictures of them."

And she did. The day after she gave the drawings to the police, they arrested Rockefeller Center, a black-eyed go-go dancer and a gasoline truck driver.

———➤●◄———

Many parents think the most important degree a girl gets from her college years isn't a "B.S. or B.A., but an M.R.S."

———➤●◄———

A sign in the local bank window read: "Come in and see us if you are loanly."

———➤●◄———

At a men's clothing store catering to fat guys, there was a sign: "Go thou and thin no more."

———➤●◄———

We once knew a woman who insisted that chewing gum was made from rubber tires. This woman had perfect teeth, never a cavity. But when she was twenty-one she began a yearly ordeal of having her teeth rotated and balanced.

———➤●◄———

Did you ever wonder why grooms don't get showers? There's a reason. He's already washed up.

The mental therapy speaker was addressing a women's club.

"You should always accentuate the positive in your life. Downplay the negative. Say "Is" rather than "not.""

After the lecture, one woman said to her friend, "I'm through making negative statements. From now on everything is positive."

"Give me an example," said her friend.

"I'm used to saying that my sloppy husband isn't fit to live with hogs. Now I'm gong to say that he is fit to live with them."

———————

Q: Did you hear of the nursing student who was made to quit school?
A: Reason: Absent too many times without gauze.

———————

One robin doesn't make a spring, but one lark can result in a fall.

———————

Dr. Jane Doe, a surgeon, was married to a guy who was undergoing a series of operations by specialists. After many years, Dr. Doe asked for a divorce, saying, "I'm sick of other people constantly opening my male."

———————

A parishioner met his clergyman on the street but didn't associate the familiar face with the church. He said, "I can't remember your name, but somehow, your faith is familiar."

———————

The young, unrecognized poet was trying to persuade a publisher to publish her poetic works.

"But, you've never published a poem...in magazines or newspapers," the publisher rejoined.

"True, but I've recited my poems to lots of folks and they loved them. Here's a letter I got last week." 'You are unquestionably one of the most promising poets in America. You have the understanding of life of Lord Byron, the verve of Longfellow, and the romantic sense of Shelley.'

"I have to admit that's a lovely testimony," the publisher said. "Who wrote it?"

"My mother," the young lady replied.

———⟶●⟵———

He was like a cock who thought the sun had risen to hear him crow.

George Eliot
Adam Bede, 1859

———⟶●⟵———

Why are women so much more interesting to men than men are to women?

Virginia Woolf
(1882-1941)

———⟶●⟵———

We were walking down the street. He looked into another girls' eyes and just fell madly in love. She was wearing mir-rored sunglasses.

———⟶●⟵———

Two secretaries were chatting in the office. One said: "Whenever my husband treats me badly, I tell him that I'll go home to my mother."

"I have a much better system. I tell him that if he doesn't tone down I'll invite my mother to come live with us."

Carol: "Where did you go on vacation last year?"
Sandy: "We went to New York."
Carol: "What hotel did you stay in?"
Sandy: "I forget the name. Paul, bring me a towel from the bathroom."

———⟫●⟪———

No healthy man is ever modest. His conversation is one endless boast — often covert, but always undiluted.

H. L. Mencken

———⟫●⟪———

If a man is vain, flatter. If timid, flatter. If beautiful, flatter. In all of history, too much flattery never lost a gentleman.

Katherine Cravens
Pursuit of a Gentleman

———⟫●⟪———

If a female deer sprouted antlers, would a male deer sprout ulcers?

———⟫●⟪———

A Dorothy Parkerism: "You may lead a horticulture but you can't make her think."

———⟫●⟪———

Jill: "Knock, knock."
Tom: "Who's there?"
Jill: "Annapolis."
Tom: "Annapolis who?"
Jill: "Annapolis is a fruit."

———⟫●⟪———

A press agent is a woman who hitches her braggin' to a star.

Diets can really be helpful to folks who are thick and tired of it all.

———⟫●⟨———

Women's lib: a Ms. is as good as a male.

———⟫●⟨———

Son Tommy told his daddy that when he grew up he wanted to be a truck driver. His dad said, "That's OK with me, Tommy, I won't stand in your way."

———⟫●⟨———

A yes man: one who stoops to conquer.

———⟫●⟨———

Two secretaries were having lunch together. "How do you like your new job?" one asked.

"It's just fine," the other answered. "And I'm sure they're going to keep me permanently."

"Oh, is that what they told you?"

"No, but yesterday the boss bought me a dictionary."

———⟫●⟨———

Doe to buck: "Let's have a little faun."

———⟫●⟨———

A woman got home loaded with packages. Her husband opened the door and yelled, "What do you mean buying all that stuff? I'll bet you spent a fortune. I hate to think of what's happened to our nest egg."

"I'll tell you what happened," his wife growled, " That old hen got tired of sitting on it."

Mary O'Brien sent a rare Christmas card reading, "Irish you a Merry Christmas."

———

Two secretaries were talking about their work. "I hate filing," said one. "No matter how careful I am, I can never find the papers I'm looking for. I forget where I have filed them."

"I used to have that problem, but no more," her friend said. "Now I make 26 copies of everything I type and file one under each letter of the alphabet. That way, I can't miss."

———

Elmer and Rosie had three daughters all wearing braces. Elmer explained: "We say that braces on our daughters is putting your money where their mouth is."

———

My psychiatrist has a patient who is a hypochondriac. She believes that life is merely a bed of neuroses.

———

Teacher to student: "Have you read any good mysteries lately?"
Student: "Yes, I'm reading one now."
Teacher: "What's the title?"
Student: "*Advanced Algebra.*"

———

The womanizer walked up to a lovely girl standing alone at the cocktail party. Using one of the oldest gambits ever, he said, "I'm Leo the Lion, what's your sign?"

"She gave him a cold stare and replied: "No trespassing!"

When Johnny Jones and his wife have a difference of opinion, his wife ends the argument with: "Are you a man or mouse...squeak up!"

———>●<———

Husband: "You were more buoyant when I was a boy."
Wife: "And you were more gallant when I was a young gal."

———>●<———

A lady dentist has this saying for her professional motto: "The tooth, the whole tooth and nothing but the tooth."

———>●<———

An old gal from Kalamazoo
Once dreamed she was eating her shoe,
She awoke late that night
In a terrible fright
Now instead of one tongue she has two.

———>●<———

Did you hear of the woman who had a doctorate in economics and taught at university level? Each day she rode to class on a business cycle.

———>●<———

A guy was asked how he had met his wife. "I met her in a travel bureau," he replied. "She was looking for a vacation, and I was the last resort."

———>●<———

The plane was about to take off when a couple were seen hugging and kissing good-bye...the flight was called at last and the two parted.

The woman sobbed bitterly as she boarded the plane and took her seat next to a little old woman, a grandmotherly type. She had seen the whole episode and said to the still-sobbing woman, "I know just how you feel: It's always tough to take leave of your husband like that."

"No, that's not it," the woman said. "It's just that I'm on my way back to him."

———◦———

Housewife: You know — sleeping maids.

———◦———

Q: How do you get your husband out of a tree?
A: Cut the rope.

———◦———

When you are in love with someone you want to be near him all the time, except when you are buying things and charging them to him.
Miss Piggy
in Henry Beard, *Miss Piggy's Guide to Life*

———◦———

No gold-digging for me...I take diamonds! We may be off the gold standard someday.
Mae West

———◦———

Love is a man's insane desire to become a woman's meal ticket.
Gideon Wurdz (and a few others)

———◦———

The trouble with some women is that they get all excited about nothing and then marry him.
Cher

Diamonds are my service stripes.

Mae West

———⟫•⟪———

The teen-aged girl had just put the latest hit album on her machine and turned the volume to the maximum, when her father came through the door. "Tell me Dad," the girl asked, "Have you heard anything to equal that great sound?"

"Only once," Dad said, "When I was a kid I saw a truck loaded with empty milk cans hit another truck loaded with hogs. The sounds were similar."

———⟫•⟪———

Two secretaries were having lunch and chatting. "All you ever talk about is money," one girl said.

"You're mistaken," the other replied. "I talk about men, too."

"What kind of men?"

"Men with money, of course!"

———⟫•⟪———

I am a marvelous housekeeper. Every time I leave a man, I keep his house.

Zsa Zsa Gabor

———⟫•⟪———

Men are like tea — the true strength and decency are not properly drawn until they have been in hot water.

Lillie Hitchcock (1843-1929)

———⟫•⟪———

The mother was having a hard time convincing her son to go to school. He was standing at the front door, crying and saying, "Everybody hates me. The kids stick their tongues out at me, the bus driver pushes me around, and the teachers talk about me. The school superintendent wants to transfer me to another school. Even the janitor won't speak to me. So, I'm not going to school today."

"Yes, you are," responded his mother. "You're now a big boy and strong and you've got a lot to learn. You got to show people you know how to take charge of your life. And what's more, you're 40-years-old and the principal. So get going!"

———⟫●⟪———

Husband: "Dearest, Honey, I've got good news and bad news. First, I've decided to run off with Crystal."
Wife: "What's the bad news?"

———⟫●⟪———

Martha: "Yesterday I got a real nice used car for my husband."
Polly: "Wonderful. It does sound like you got a good trade."

———⟫●⟪———

A husband is what is left of a lover after the nerve has been extracted.

> Helen Rowland
> *A Guide to Men*, 1922

———⟫●⟪———

One vacation day, the father was showing his six-year-old a photograph of her mother's wedding and telling her what a great day it was for them as well as grandpa and grandma and all their friends attending the wedding.

"Glad to see all this, Daddy. That was the day Mama came to work for us, wasn't it?"

———⟫●⟪———

Conran's law of housework — it expands to fill all the time available to you plus forty-five minutes.

The woman received her final divorce decree from her husband, a composer of music and songwriter. She was talking things over with her friend.

"You know, dear, I told you not to marry him," her friend said. "Those guys who are musicians and write music make the worst husbands. I told you so."

Six months later the divorced woman married another songwriter. The following day she got a note from her first husband saying, "All the best and congratulations." It was signed, "THE FRYING PAN!"

I wouldn't kidnap a man for sex — I'm not saying I couldn't use someone to oil the lawnmower.

Victoria Wood
1953

'Tis strange what a man may do, and a woman yet think him an angel.

William Makepeace Thackery
(1811-1863)

Two women were discussing their daughters who were away at college.

"What does your daughter plan to do when she graduates?" one woman asked.

"I'm not sure," the other replied. "Judging from her letters to me she'd make an excellent professional fund raiser."

On being asked what is the difference between man and woman, he answered: I can't conceive.

John Pentland Mahaffy
(1839-1919)

When women go wrong, men go right after them.
                                                 Mae West
                                              (1892-1980)

A husband came home from work to find his wife sobbing before the television set. "How on earth can you get so worked-up over the troubles of those people in the soaps when you don't even know them?"

"I guess it's the same thing that causes you to scream and get excited when men you don't know grab a ball and chase one another up and down the field!"

"How come you're so generous with little things like leaving your brain to science?"

"It's sure sad about Ginny," one woman said to another. "Since she lost all her money, half of her friends have deserted her."

"Yeah, what about the other half?" her friend asked.

"They don't know she's broke!" was the reply.

———————

When asked by Hedda Hopper, the gossip columnist, how she knew so much about men, Mae West replied: "Baby, I went to night school."

———————

The best way to hold a man is in your arms.

Mae West
(1892-1980)

———————

Day after day the woman's husband would watch the football games on television while she did housework. One day, while he was watching TV and the game, she got real mad and yelled at him: "Hey, you! If I should fall off this step-ladder would you mind calling an ambulance during half-time?"

———————

A man has nine hundred dollars and you leave him with two dollars, that's subtraction.

Mae West
(1892-1980)

The female sex has no greater fan than I, and I have the bills to prove it.

Alan Jay Lerner
(1918-1986)

An addicted horse player hadn't been to church for years. Finally his wife persuaded him to go.

On the way home, he said to her: "I rather enjoyed it. Nice pews, good choir, and did you notice that people looked at me when I joined the choir with my great, deep bass voice?"

"Yeah, I noticed," his wife replied. "But next time we go, and you sing, be sure that you sing 'Hallelujah, Hallelujah' and not 'Hialeah, Hialeah!'"

The Panama Canal locks opened in 1914 but its developers forgot the cream cheese.

The installation of the first mail box was inevitable. Everyone knew it would happen sooner or letter.

Dirty dishes filled the sink, the kid's clothes and toys and books made a shambles of every room. And dinner wasn't ready.

"What in the world has happened to my house?" he asked his wife.

"Not a thing. Nothing! You are always wondering what I do the live-long day. Well, take a look. Today I didn't do it."

My daughter the vegetable gardener mailed her bulk shipments by parsley post.

Colleges have finally started to give marriage courses. The reason? To give students a good wed-ucation.

———————

It was pouring rain and the housewife decided to call a cab to go to the supermarket. As luck had it, one of the cabs was right in front of the woman's house so that when the cab driver heard the request on his radio, he merely had to stop and there he was in front of her house.

When the lady entered his cab, he said, "Isn't that fast service ma'am?"

With a look of surprise she said, getting out of the cab, "I wouldn't dare ride with anybody who drives as fast as you do!" Then she slammed the door and left!

———————

The first women allowed in the Navy later became the first permanent WAVE.

———————

The invention of the straight pin ended with several people getting stuck-up.

———————

Two women were discussing the energy crisis and one asked the other: "Which of our natural resources do you think will be gone first?"

"The taxpayer," was the other's reply.

———————

The teacher was trying to impress her students with doing school work properly. "Just remember, children, that work well done never has to be done over again."

"If that's so, what about when I mow the lawn?" responded one boy.

The invention of soda was greeted by the inventor's daughter, saying: "That's my Pop!"

———›◦‹———

You probably won't believe it but dental floss was invented in 1938. Honest! That's the tooth.

———›◦‹———

The woman got a phone call that told her of an emergency that involved her husband. She had to reach her daughter who had the car and was attending a cooking class. But Mom didn't know where the cooking class was held, knew only that the teacher was named Johnson. So, she looked in the phone book to discover that there were 24 Johnsons listed. She started with the first one and a voice answered. "Pardon me," the woman said, "Is this the Johnson home where a teenage girl is attending the cooking class?"

"No," the woman said, "This is the Johnson home where the woman was taking a shower."

———›◦‹———

The people who created the maternity ward were probably responsible for the development of the stork market.

———›◦‹———

The first thermometer was invented by a lady scientist with many degrees.

———›◦‹———

Sally Jane bought a high-powered, brand new convertible. She asked her priest to give it his blessing. The priest then cautioned: "Just remember, Sally Jane, that this blessing is no good above fifty miles an hour."

A druggist said to an old customer: "Edie, did that mud-pack I sold you last week improve your husband's complexion and appearance?"

"It did for a couple of days," was the reply, "but then it wore off!"

—————

When the woman who invented the elastic girdle was asked, "Does it work?" She replied: "Of corset does."

—————

When the first windows were installed in the town's new skyscraper they were thought to be a pain in the glass.

—————

An oil-rich fellow in Dallas, Texas had his cute, blonde secretary out for dinner and was half-way through the meal when his wife popped in the door, saw him, frowned and left! When she got home she called the Dallas newspaper and told the obituary editor: "My husband died. Please tell your readers."

"When did he die, Ma'am?" the editor asked.

"He starts tomorrow," was the reply.

—————

Men's role is uncertain, undefined, and perhaps unnecessary. By a great effort man has hit upon a method of compensating himself for his basic inferiority.

                                        Margaret Mead

—————

A lady who makes a living as a photo finisher once remarked: "Someday my prints will come."

—————

Women who put candles on their birthday cake merely want to make light of their age.

In 1850 the first dressmaker shop opened. From the first it seamed to do well.

———⊃>●≪⊂———

The turn of the century saw the first submarine sandwich. The company went under, unfortunately.

———⊃>●≪⊂———

In our scrutiny of (400 years of flagellant literature), certain patterns emerge. Primarily we find the most enthusiastic recipients of whipping are men. It becomes further evident that most self-respecting flagellants prefer to have the operation performed on them by women. Since the majority of flagellants seem to enjoy their work thoroughly, this makes for a very satisfactory arrangement.

               Bernhardt J. Hurwood
               The Golden Age of Erotia, 1965

———⊃>●≪⊂———

The comfortable estate of widowhood is the only hope that keeps up a wife's spirits.

               John Gay
               The Beggars Opera,
               1728

———⊃>●≪⊂———

Someone asked: "Why do people buy jogging machines?" The reply was: "They hope to get a run for their money."

———⊃>●≪⊂———

It was as recent as 1945 that card playing in the USA reached the pinochle of success.

———⊃>●≪⊂———

Do you know what dresses were called in the twenties? They were called "dogs" because you could peek-on-knees.

Marriage is a feast where the grace is sometimes better than the dinner.

Charles Caleb Colton
(1780-1832)

———>●<———

Nowadays, two can live as cheaply as one large family used to!

Joey Adams

———>●<———

Friendships, like marriages, are dependent on avoiding the unforgivable.

John D. MacDonald

———>●<———

Almost all married people fight, although many are ashamed to admit it. Actually a marriage in which no quarreling at all takes place may well be one that is dead or dying from emotional undernourishment. If you care, you probably fight.

Flora Davis

———>●<———

Often the difference between a successful marriage and a mediocre one consists of leaving about three or four things a day unsaid.

Harlan Miller

———>●<———

A woman who was head over heels in debt got a letter from one of her creditors. "Dear Madam, please pay something on your overdue account. We have been extremely patient with you. In fact, we've been more considerate of you than your own mother. We've carried you for eleven months."

"Why an examination? I explained fully to you what's wrong with him!"

Receptionists

You've got a long wait ahead of you when the receptionist says, "He's at a meeting, but you're welcome to have a seat and wait. May I bring you a cup of tea and perhaps a pillow and blanket?"

Receptionists should keep in mind that it costs no more to be pleasant to visitors. And if it did, it certainly wouldn't be reflected in your paycheck.

Receptionists should be outgoing, friendly, courteous, kind and validate parking.

———>●<———

Some receptionists are always pleasant simply because they don't know what the heck is going on in the office. Yet other receptionists are grumpy simply because they're the only ones who do know what the heck is going on in the office.

———>●<———

Secretaries

Even though it may sound blasphemous, God is not all-seeing, all-knowing, and all-powerful. His secretary is behind it all.

———>●<———

God is like all the bosses. He does all things except make His own coffee in the office.

———>●<———

God gives us all our blessings, but His secretary shops around for them.

———>●<———

Secretaries are merely training wheels of executives.

———>●<———

Two of the most miserable sights in the business world are a briefcase without a handle and an executive minus a secretary.

An executive without a secretary is like a turtle without a shell...except the turtle moves faster.

...also gets more done.

———>➤●❤<———

When the boss doesn't show up for work, the secretary finds lots to do.

When the secretary doesn't show up for work, the boss has trouble finding his own chair.

———>➤●❤<———

Every executive needs an efficient secretary. It's either that or he has to learn to dial the phone himself.

———>➤●❤<———

If every secretary walked out, business would not shut down. But nobody would get any coffee.

...Well, not any really good coffee.

———>➤●❤<———

And no boss would have a lunch reservation.

———>➤●❤<———

A good secretary can do lots more than type and take dictation. A good secretary can create the illusion that the boss is truly in charge.

———>➤●❤<———

A good secretary can manipulate the boss without ever letting him see the magical strings.

———>➤●❤<———

One secretary finally refused to answer the phone for her boss. She said, "Four out of five times it's for you, anyway."

Napoleon Bonaparte once said to his secretary, "You, too, will be immortal."

She said, "Why?"

He said, "Because you are Napoleon's secretary."

She said, "Really? Give me the name of Julius Caesar's secretary."

———>●<———

An executive was dictating a letter to his secretary. He said, "Take this letter to the firm of Simmons, Lasker, & Bolton. Dear Gentlemen..."

The secretary said, "Boss, I hate to contradict you, but I've dated all three of those jerks, and not a darn one of them is a gentleman."

———>●<———

I wouldn't marry anyone I fell in love with at our office. We have lousy control in our company.

———>●<———

They kiss all the way home from work. That's difficult since he drives a Ford Mustang and she drives a Dodge.

———>●<———

There's also the office Romeo. He told one fellow worker he was God's gift to women. She said, "I don't think so. God would have wrapped you better."

———>●<———

This office Don Juan has two goals in life: to try to make every woman in the office, and to find a cure for staple-gun wounds.

———>●<———

This guy is single and deserves it, too.

Many love affairs begin in the office. That's where I first fell in love with cash.

———>>●<<———

He's not really good looking, either. In fact, he looks surprisingly like the drawings of him on the wall in the women's washroom.

———>>●<<———

Office Romance

Sometimes office love affairs are hard to resist. They're joyous, they're delightful, and they're on company time.

———>>●<<———

I know a man who was very proud that he was faithful to his wife...and several of his office playmates.

———>>●<<———

It's hard to avoid love affairs in some offices. The Muzak is so romantic.

———>>●<<———

They first met by the office Xerox machine. It led them to mutual reproduction.

———>>●<<———

A delivery boy once had to deliver a package to Mr. Sexhauer in the accounting department of a large corporation.

When he came into the reception area, an attractive woman behind the desk said, "May I help you?"

The boy asked, "Is there a Sexhauer here?"

She said, "Pal, we don't even have a coffee break."

The boss came into work early one morning and found his bookkeeper in a passionate embrace with his secretary. The boss said, "Is that what I pay you for?" The bookkeeper said, "No, sir. I don't get paid for this. It's free of charge."

———————

Passionate romance in the executive office can be dangerous. Sex was not designed for rotating chairs.

———————

The CEO of a large manufacturing firm was a young, dynamic, executive. To stay in shape, he kept a bicycle in the parking lot and would ride that around the complex.

One day he discovered his bicycle was stolen.

It infuriated him so much that he organized a meeting of all the workers. He told an associate that he was going to give a scathing speech on ethics and morality. He was going to go back to basics. He planned to go through each of the ten commandments one by one with brief comments on each.

When he got to the Eighth Commandment, though — "Thou shalt not steal" — he would deliver an elegant, persuasive lecture. He felt this would so move the listeners that whoever stole his bicycle would surely return it.

He gave an elegant, persuasive speech, so elegant and persuasive that it put him in mind of the Eighth Commandment — and then he remembered where he'd left the bicycle.

———————

One boss used to warn all his male employees against inter-office affairs by saying, "Never dip your own pen in company ink."

———————

Management demands that sex should not be had in the office. They don't hold committee meetings in your bedroom, do they?

Many executives religiously refrain from sex while on the job. They prefer to be incompetent at one thing at a time.

―――――→●←―――――

Some workplaces have managed to eliminate sex in the office. They have the thermostats in the office sprinkler system set very low.

―――――→●←―――――

Office advice: "Leave reproduction in the office to the copying machines."

―――――→●←―――――

One behind-the-times company finally promoted a woman to top management, and some of the members of that formerly all-male establishment resented it.

One member was particularly discourteous to his new colleague. She confronted him.

He said, "I may be old fashioned, but I'm offended by your executive position here. I'm embarrassed by it. I feel the same way I would if you intruded on me while I was naked in my own bedroom and had nothing to defend myself with."

She said, "Relax. You're not good looking enough to have those kind of worries, nor armed strongly enough."

―――――→●←―――――

Sir Thomas Beecham was a renowned conductor and founder of the London Philharmonic Orchestra. However, he was also like some of today's managers.

Someone asked once if it was true that he preferred *not* to have women in his orchestra.

He said, "The problem is, if they're attractive it will upset my players. If they're not it upsets me."

―――――→●←―――――

The boss called his secretary into the office and said, "We've got to stop our affair. If I spend any more money on you, my wife might find out."

The secretary said, "If you don't spend more money on me, you can be sure she will."

"My dad is gonna pay for it. But he brought my mom along because she haggles better!"

There's a story told that Noah Webster, who compiled Webster's American Dictionary of the English Language in 1828, was caught in an embrace with his secretary when his wife unexpectedly walked into his study.

The wife said, "Why, Noah, I'm surprised."

Webster said, "No, my dear, I'm surprised; you're astonished."

You know the kind of girl. She was 28 years old before she found out that drive-ins showed movies.

———— >≫●≪< ————

She wears mini-skirts that are so short the only thing they don't show is her nationality.

———— >≫●≪< ————

She's a real office cutie pie. She has a walk that says: "To whom it may concern."

———— >≫●≪< ————

She has a seductive walk. She's one of those girls who can wink at you while she walks away from you.

———— >≫●≪< ————

Around the office she's known as the girl most likely to concede.

———— >≫●≪< ————

She wears so much make-up, she has to get a friend to help her smile. In her purse she carried a clay pack and putty knife.

———— >≫●≪< ————

THE OFFICE DON JUAN:

There's usually one guy in every office who thinks he's God's gift to women. And the women think: If he is, then God's one lousy dry goods buyer.

———— >≫●≪< ————

They think, "If this guy is God's gift to women, I sure hope God kept the receipts."

This guy keeps saying to the female employees, "Wouldn't you like to get me in bed?" And they say, "Yes, once there, we can smother you with a pillow."

———>∙∘∙<———

This guy has a one-track mind, and that track is all dirt.

———>∙∘∙<———

If it weren't for impure thoughts, this guy would have no thoughts at all.

———>∙∘∙<———

If he sends a box of candy, he doesn't consider it a gift; he considers it a contract and acceptance.

———>∙∘∙<———

Women generally dislike this guy. In an unofficial office poll, he finished lower than cracker crumbs as things they would least likely like to wind up in bed with.

———>∙∘∙<———

He is a generous fellow and offers his body to everyone and so far the only ones who have accepted are the people at the city organ bank.

———>∙∘∙<———

This gentleman usually lives in a world of his own. From any attractive woman, he considers "Good morning" a proposition.

———>∙∘∙<———

There was the guy who was held up by a bandit. "Your money or your life," the bandit said. "Take my life," the guy replied, "I'm saving my money for my old age."

Definition of a pedestrian: A man with two cars — one driven by his wife, the other by one of his children.

—————➤●◄—————

She's descended from a long line her mother listened to.

Gypsy Rose Lee

—————➤●◄—————

A woman went to her doctor and asked for help to go to sleep at night and not snore. Snoring was her big problem. "As soon as I go to sleep, I start to snore. Every time. Can you help me?"

"Does it bother your husband?" the doctor asked.

"Not only him! But it upsets the entire congregation."

—————➤●◄—————

The reason grandparents and grandchildren get along so well is that they have a common enemy.

Sam Levinson

—————➤●◄—————

Never let a panty hose line show around your ankles.

Joan Rivers

—————➤●◄—————

A woman was returning to the United States from Europe and the customs inspector asked her if she had anything to declare. "Only my own clothing," she replied.

"I have to check your bag," the inspector told her and opened the suitcase and found a bottle of scotch. "What about this?" the officer asked. "You told me you had nothing but clothing."

"That's right," she replied. "That's my nightcap!"

———>⮞◉⮜<———

I adore the lines the men use to get us into bed: "Please, it will only take a minute." What am I...a microwave?

Beverly Mickens

———>⮞◉⮜<———

A woman gets on the train with her son and gives the conductor one ticket. "How old is your kid?" the conductor asked. The mother replied, "He's five years old."

"He looks not less than twelve to me," the conductor said.

"Can I help it if he worries?" the woman replied.

———>⮞◉⮜<———

There are several ways to apportion a family's income, all of them unsatisfactory.

Robert Benchley

———>⮞◉⮜<———

Americans are getting stronger. Twenty years ago it took two people to carry ten dollars worth of groceries. Today any five-year-old can do it.

Henny Youngman

———>⮞◉⮜<———

You have to stay in shape. My grandmother started walking five miles a day when she was sixty. She's ninety-seven today and we don't know where the hell she is.

Ellen Degeneres

Whatever you have read I have said is almost certainly untrue, except if it is funny in which case I definitely said it.

                                            Tallulah Bankhead

———➤●◄———

Two girls were having lunch in a restaurant and one had ordered and was eating a cottage cheese sandwich. The other asked: "Are you on a low calorie diet?"

"Not a low calorie diet, but a low salary diet."

———➤●◄———

There once was a lady named psyche
Whose love was a fellow named Yche.
But the thing about Yche
That the girl didn't lyche
Was his beard that was dreadfully pspyche

———➤●◄———

Two old friends were talking over coffee. "I'm so glad that you decided against a divorce from George," the one girl said.

"Well, it was this way. We decided to stay together because of the children. George wouldn't take them and neither would I."

———➤●◄———

The judge was talking to the woman who had sued for divorce. "You state in your complaint that you need a divorce because of poor health. Would you explain that, please?"

"It's quite simple, Your Honor. I just got mighty sick of having him around the house."

———➤●◄———

A lady who rules St. Montgomery
Says the wearing of clothes is mere mummery.
She has frequently tea'd in

The costumes of Eden,
appearing delightfully summery.

——————>⊃●⊂——————

The new bride giggled and told her friend: "My husband is very good to me. I only have to ask for something and he gets it for me."

Her friend replied: "That just goes to show you ain't asking for enough."

——————>⊃●⊂——————

I've been asked to say a couple of words about my husband, Fang. How about "short" and "cheap."

Phyllis Diller

——————>⊃●⊂——————

What counts is not how many animals were killed to get the fur, but how many animals the woman had to sleep with to get the fur.

Angela La Greca

——————>⊃●⊂——————

My good friend is always feeling sad on Father's Day, mainly because he has no children.

"Did you have an unhappy life at home?"

"No, we were quite happy. My wife laughed at everything I did. That's why we have no children."

——————>⊃●⊂——————

I never sees men or dogs but what I ache to kill them.

August Main
arrested for murder, 1897

——————>⊃●⊂——————

A good part — and definitely the most fun part — of being a feminist is about frightening men. American and Australian feminists have always known this...of course, there's a lot more to feminism but scaring the shit out of the scumbags is an amusing and necessary part because, sadly, a good many men respect nothing but strength.

> Julia Burchill
> British Columnist, 1989

There once lived a teacher named Dodd
with manners arresting and odd.
She said: "If you please
Spell my name with three d's
Though one was sufficient for God.

"Now I'd like to advise you of YOUR rights...you have the right to know that the chief of police is my husband!"

Masters Agency

CHAPTER SEVEN

The only medicine that needs no prescription, has no unpleasant taste, and costs no money is laughter.

If you want to sacrifice the admiration of many men for the criticism of one, go ahead, get married.

> Katherine Hepburn
> Quoting her mother, Katherine
> Houghton Hepburn, 1928

Every woman should have a man for love, companionship and sympathy, preferably at three different locations.

It doesn't matter what you do in the bedroom as long as you don't do it in the street and frighten the horses.

> Mrs. Patrick Campbell
> 1910

There was a young lady from Lynn
Who happened to sit on a pin.
But to add to her contour
She'd stuck so much on tour
The point didn't puncture the skynne.

A cop came to the scene of an automobile accident and saw a woman lying unconscious near the automobile. A man was trying to revive the woman.

"Who was driving the car?" the policeman asked.

"I was," said the man who was helping the woman.

"How did you hit her?" the cop asked.

"But I didn't hit her," the guy replied. "As I came to the intersection, I noticed her trying to cross the street. So I stopped for her and she fainted."

———⟫●⟪———

The only men who are too young are the ones who write love letters in crayon, wear pajamas with feet, or fly half fare.

Phyllis Diller

———⟫●⟪———

There was a young girl from St. Paul
Wore a newspaper dress to a ball
But the dress caught on fire
and burned her entire
front page-sporting section-and all.

———⟫●⟪———

Such idealistic sentiments presumed that men were educable, even though ten thousand years of experience have shown that they are not.

———⟫●⟪———

Sometimes I think if there were a third sex, men wouldn't get as much as a glance from me.

Amanda Wail
Love Me Little
1958

———⟫●⟪———

Genius has no sex.

Germaine DeStael
1810

The main difference between men and women is that men are lunatics and women are idiots.

Raphael West

———>●<———

A father and son were in the living room while mom and daughter were in the kitchen cleaning up after supper.

There came a loud crash from the kitchen. They waited but heard not a sound or voice.

"Mom just broke some dishes," the boy announced.

"But how do you know?" asked father.

"Because she isn't saying a darn thing," the boy replied.

———>●<———

A woman said to her best friend: "I don't think I look like age 50, do you?"

Her friend replied, "No, but you used to."

———>●<———

A young woman, recently married, called the newspaper and asked for the food editor.

"Please help me," she said to the food editor. "My mother-in-law and her husband are coming to a special dinner tomorrow night and I need to have a perfect dinner for them. I bought a ten-pound turkey but I wonder if you could tell me how long to cook it?"

"Just a minute," said the editor as he began to check his reference book. He put the phone down so quickly that he didn't hear the woman on the other end of the line say, "Oh, thank you very much. You've been a very big help."

———>●<———

There was a young girl in the choir
Whose voice went up hoir and hoir,
Till one Sunday night
It vanished from sight
And they found it next day in the spoir.

The neighbor said, "You really must pull your shades at night. Last night I looked towards your house and saw you making love to your wife."

"Ha, Ha!" the man laughed. "The joke's on you. I wasn't even home last night."

———————

At a bridge party several women were talking. One, who was suspected of hiding her age, said with a sad face, "My goodness but I hate to think of life after 40."

One of her friends said, "Why?" What happened to you then?"

———————

Several years ago, two youngsters were trying to talk their grandmother into taking her first airplane ride.

"Not me!" she said, "I'm going to sit here and enjoy television like the good Lord intended."

———————

"How is your marriage working out?" her friend asked. "It's my understanding that one problem with marrying a widower is that he wants to talk about his earlier wife. Do you have that problem?"

"At first I did. But I cured him of it."

"How on earth did you manage to do that?" she was asked.

"Whenever he began to talk about his previous wife, I began to talk about my next husband."

———————

A strip tease named Cubbard in Kansas
Said, "Mine's a routine that entrances."
But when censors got there
Miss Cubbard was bare
She explained, "I don't know where my fans is."

A young woman had just graduated from college, had received a fine job with a large corporation located in New York and she had settled in her new apartment. Next on her agenda was a new car. She went to her bank and was in process of arranging the loan. When all her papers were in order, she told the banker: "It's been good working with you. How can I thank you enough for what you've done for me?"

"That's easy," replied the banker. "Monthly, that's all. Just pay monthly is the way to thank me."

———————

Any girl can be glamorous; all you have to do is stand still and act stupid.

Hedy Lemar

———————

It isn't that gentlemen really prefer blondes, it's just that we look dumber.

Anita Loos
1894-1981

———————

Men are always ready to respect anything that bores them.

Marilyn Monroe
1926-1962

———————

A student from dear old Bryn Mawr
Committed a dreadful faux pas
She loosened a stay
In her new decollete
Exposing her jene sais quoi.

———————

God made men stronger but not necessarily more intelligent. He gave women intuition and femininity, and then used

241

properly, that combination easily jumbles the brain of any man I ever met.

Farah Fawcett

———>●<———

And now for that old favorite: Men seldom make passes at girls who wear glasses.

Dorothy Parker
Enough Rope
1926

———>●<———

Find me an obviously intelligent man, a man free from sentimentality and illusion, a man hard to deceive, a man of the first class and I'll show you a man with a wide streak of woman in him. The caveman is all muscles and mush. Without a woman to rule him and think for him, he is a truly lamentable spectacle: a baby with whiskers, a rabbit with the frame of anairochs, a feeble and preposterous caricature of God.

———>●<———

I like a lawyer, even more
   I prefer a physician,
But I admit I'd die before
   I'd send for a mortician.

———>●<———

Cyd Charisse had this to say about men: "Treat as a pet. Three meals a day, plenty of affection, a loose leash and do not disturb while eating."

———>●<———

Did you hear about the cheapskate husband who took his pregnant wife to the supermarket because he heard they had free delivery?

Q: What are the worst five years in the life of a Nebraska man?
A: The fifth grade.

———➤●◄———

As a beauty, I'm not a great star,
There are others more handsome by far.
But my face, I don't mind it,
Because I'm behind it
It's the people in front that I jar.

———➤●◄———

Did you hear about the old lady from Tarentum?
There was an old lady from Tarentum
Who gnashed her false teeth till she bent 'em,
when asked what they cost
and how much she'd lost —
She said, "I don't know. I just rent 'em."

———➤●◄———

Speaking of dentures, did you hear this one?
Two comics were having dinner when one says: "I'm dining tomorrow with the upper set.　Some class, eh?"
Comic number two replied: "The steak may be tough. Best to take your lowers, too."

———➤●◄———

There was an old lady of Whiteheath
Who sat on her very own false teeth.
Said she with a cry,
"I should use my eye —
Here I've bitten myself underneath."

———➤●◄———

There was a nurse at Memorial Hospital who constantly referred to her patient as "The Old Sardine."

The supervisor asked her one day why she said that.

"That's easy to explain," she said. "Stay here for an hour and see how many times he wants to go to the can."

———>●<———

A physician asked his client: "Was your husband seriously hurt in the accident?"

"Yes, sure he was," was her reply. "He suffered from conclusion of the brain."

"I think you mean concussion of the brain, don't you?"

"Nope," responded the woman, "I meant what I said. 'Conclusion.' He's dead."

———>●<———

Usually, this wolfish kind of guy is a bad grammarian. He ends every sentence with a proposition.

———>●<———

A woman stopped at a resort hotel and asked the price of rooms. "Rooms on the first floor are $100, on the second floor they are $90, on the third floor they're $80."

The woman shook her head and started to leave. "Aren't you going to stay with us?" the clerk asked. "Isn't our hotel attractive enough for you?"

"Yes, it's quite attractive," she answered, "but it's just not tall enough for me."

———>●<———

A woman and her friend were discussing the forthcoming trip to Yellowstone Park that one of them was about to take.

"When you get to Yellowstone," her friend advised, "don't forget Old Faithful."

"Don't worry! I'll not forget. I'm taking him with me."

———>●<———

Two guys: One of them says: "You're calling on that widow every night. Why not marry her?"

"If I do, where will I spend my evenings?"

Mother heard her five-year-old daughter screaming in the next room and rushed there to see what the trouble was. The little girl sat there while her brother pulled her hair with all his might.

"Don't let it bother you," the mother said, "Your little brother doesn't know what he's doing."

A few minutes after the mom left the room, she heard more screaming. This time she found the baby brother in tears.

"What's wrong with Emil?" Mother asked.

"Not much," the little girl said, "But now he knows!"

———⇒>●<⇐———

"How's that used car you bought last week?" a woman asked her friend.

"It's awful," her friend responded. "You never in your life heard so many rattles. Everything on it makes noise except the horn."

"You say I'm overdrawn — I say you're underdeposited."

Masters Agency

Cadence: A stupid girl named Kay.

Arson: Our daughter's brother.

Dogma: A mother dog.

Hunger: What the posse did to the lady rustler.

Hypothesis: The first thing a daughter says to her father on the telephone.

———————

A good and true husband remembers his wife's birthdays but forgets her age.

———————

The noisy audience was so disturbing to the speaker that, after four or five minutes of total frustration, he pounded on the lectern and shouted into the microphone: "May I have a bit of quiet! You are making so much noise that I can't hear a word of what I'm saying!"

A lady in the room shouted up to him, "Don't worry, Mister, you ain't missing a thing."

———————

Two women were discussing a local politician. "Did you hear his last speech?" one of them asked. "I sure did," the other replied, "and I hope it truly is his last."

———————

The young woman had been shopping for clothes for her Caribbean cruise about to take place. She was showing her mother what she'd bought. When she showed her mother the new bikini, her mother said, "If I'd had one of those when I was your age, you'd be four years older than you are."

———————

Husband to wife: "What a dress! That's the funniest rag I ever saw and I'm still laughing at it."

Wife to husband: "If you think you're laughing now, wait till you get the bill and see what it cost you!"

━━━➤●◄━━━

At the dinner table, Mother was talking to her little kids about the Ten Commandments. "Can you kids tell me the Commandment that has only four words?" she asked.

Her little girl said, "I can, Mommy. It's 'keep off the grass'!"

━━━➤●◄━━━

Two youngsters were discussing Sunday School and one asked, "Do you believe in the devil?"

"Not at all," the other replied, "It's just like Christmas and Santa Clause. It's your Daddy!"

━━━➤●◄━━━

In the morning the husband had a terrible fight with his wife. When he got home that night, he found a note: "Your dinner is on page 230 and your night snack is on page 52 in the cookbook. Bon appetite!"

━━━➤●◄━━━

A man and his wife were visiting Washington, D.C. with their two children. A tour guide was taking them around town and as they came up Pennsylvania Avenue, the guide said, "On your right is the National Archives building. Please notice the inscription over the entrance that says, 'The Past Is Prologue'."

"What does that mean, Mommy?" one of the kids asked.

"Translated, that means, 'You ain't seen nothin' yet'!"

━━━➤●◄━━━

Husband who likes to drink whiskey to his wife: "Honey, it makes me wonder where our boy got his thirst for knowledge."

Wife: "I can tell you. The knowledge came from me, the thirst from you!"

247

"You look just like my husband number four," a woman said to her partner at a card game.

"Really? And how many husbands have you had?" he asked.

"Three."

—————>●<—————

The high school basketball team had lost the state championship and the entire team was dejected and depressed.

Trying to cheer them up, the coach said, "You can't win 'em all. Even great men have to be second once in awhile."

"Then what about George Washington?" one player asked. "He was the first in war, first in peace, first in the hearts of his countrymen."

"That's right," said the coach, "But remember, he married a widow."

—————>●<—————

A woman told her friend, "I've had a terrible day. I chased all over town all day trying to get something for my hubby."

"Did you have many offers?" her friend asked.

—————>●<—————

What's your judgment of the women's lib movement?" one lady asked another.

"I rather think I'd like to be liberated," the one girl replied. "But first I would like to be captured."

—————>●<—————

A little old lady spoke to a guy while buying stamps at the post office.

"Do me a favor, young man," she asked, "Please address this envelope for me."

The man did just that and then the lady asked him to write a short message on a sheet of paper that she gave him. He did that, too, and then said, "Is there anything else I can do for you?"

"Yes, do please write at the bottom of my letter: 'Please excuse the awful handwriting.'"

"Didn't I tell you not to rush things on your first date?"

A first grade teacher had her class at the local zoo. In turn, each child was given a chance at guessing the names of the zoo animals. The camel, lion, giraffe, and bear and elephant all were named correctly.

"Now it's your turn," teacher said to a little girl. She pointed to a deer and asked, "What is the name of that animal?"

The little girl seemed at a loss to describe or name the animal. Finally the teacher, wanting to help her, asked,

"Think hard! What does your mother call your papa at home?"

"So that's what a baboon looks like!" the little girl exclaimed.

———➤●◄———

One way a girl can stop a guy from making love to her is to marry him.

———➤●◄———

A beautiful model came back to her office, scowling. "What's the matter, Sally?" her friend asked. "Didn't you like your new job with that illustrator?"

"I sure didn't," she replied. "He was tall, dark and all hands."

———➤●◄———

A main reason for so much divorce is because there are too many husbands and wives and not enough married couples.

———➤●◄———

We heard that a New York army unit was out to punish a New York show girl. It seems she had been contributing to the delinquency of a major.

———➤●◄———

The happiest wife is not the one who marries the excellent man but the one who makes an excellent man out of the man she married.

———➤●◄———

A young girl, working in the department store's shoe department, was waiting on a man who was very hard to please. She showed him pair after pair and finally said, "Please let me rest a minute, sir, your feet are killing me."

Marriage is not a word but a sentence.

H.L. Mencken

————⟫●⟪————

How comes it that a girl is anxious to get married and exchange an eight-hour day for a fourteen-hour day.

————⟫●⟪————

A small boy entered a woman's ready-to-wear shop and asked if he could buy his mother a slip for her birthday. "Glad to help you," a clerk told him. "What size does your Mother wear?"

"I don't know," the boy said, "but she's just perfect." The clerk wrapped up a size 34 for him.

A couple of days later, the mother came into the store and exchanged the slip for a size 52.

————⟫●⟪————

The beautiful brunette sauntered through the hotel lobby in downtown Dallas where she encountered a famous oil well operator. "Howdy, stranger," she said to him, "How much did you say your name was?"

————⟫●⟪————

Give a husband enough rope and he'll want to skip.

————⟫●⟪————

The surest way to keep a husband is in doubt.

————⟫●⟪————

One time a pregnant woman left her husband parked outside the doctor's office while she went inside for her examination. The doctor told her she would have twins and insisted her husband come to the office so he could tell him the good news. The nurse went downstairs and managed to drag the husband up to the doctor's office where the furious husband barked, "What's the idea of dragging me up here? I'll probably get a ticket for being double-parked."

"Well, young man," said the doctor, "Your wife is facing the same situation inside."

Masters Agency

Man has his will, but woman has her way.

Oliver Wendell Holmes

One of the chief reasons that widowers get married so quickly is because they find out that it bankrupts them to pay for the work that a wife does for her board and clothes.

Dorothy Dix

Puns! Puns! Puns!

I know a lingerie manufacturer who gave his wife the slip.

————————

She was the only breadwinner and she couldn't afford to loaf.

————————

The tattoo artist had designs on her clients.

————————

Way back when, even then, the Greek maidens were tired of listening to lyres.

————————

The fortuneteller said she liked her work because she always had a ball.

————————

When a guy tried to get fresh with a librarian, she threw the book at him.

————————

Most housewives hate to be tied down to housework because they are afraid they might become stir-crazy.

————————

She was only a necktie salesgirl but she knew how to collar her man.

————————

The beginning of a dog's life usually starts with some poor girl experiencing puppy love.

When two ladies, both musicians, met to discuss recent surgery, they wound up giving an organ recital.

———>∘∘<———

The judge couldn't be disturbed at her dinner because her honor was at steak.

———>∘∘<———

Mary Swanson, a hotel executive says, "All good hotel employees should be inn-experienced.

———>∘∘<———

Some ill-bred children appear on their pest behavior in company.

———>∘∘<———

My wife bought me a size 15 shirt for my birthday, but I wear a size 17, still, the gift left me all choked up.

———>∘∘<———

When Mary Hennepin saw all the grey hair she had, she thought she'd dye.

———>∘∘<———

Some women think it takes a lotta gile to land a spouse.

———>∘∘<———

At a restaurant, I looked out the window and saw some women marching down the street carrying large signs. "Is that a women's lib group?" I asked the waiter.
"I don't know," he replied, "But it more resembles the March of Dames."

———>∘∘<———

When two egotistical women meet, it's an "I" for an "I".

Did you hear about the woman who was invited to a wedding in Atlantic City just when the gambling casinos opened and they threw dice at the bride and groom?

―――――

Puns! Puns! And More Puns!

A girl at Bennington named Louise
weighted down with Ph. D.'s and D.D.'s
collapsed from the strain.
Said her doctor; "It's plain
You are killing yourself by degrees."

―――――

"Dear, you've lost your birth control pills," Tom said pregnantly.

―――――

"No, Eve, I won't touch that apple," said Tom adamantly.

―――――

"Why don't you try on these panties?" Ned said transparently.

―――――

There once was a restaurant that served only women. It featured Miss steaks.

―――――

Back in those days when miniskirts first became popular, many husbands said: "The thigh's the limit."

―――――

"My idea of a collective noun is...a garbage can," said one errant husband to his wife.

The first couple to get married as astronauts were known as Mister and Missile.

―――――>●<―――――

The first broom invented made its inventor so tired he went to sweep.

―――――>●<―――――

The first oil used for cooking was invented on Fry Day.

―――――>●<―――――

Julia Childs, on TV, says she writes to her cooking school classmates as her pan pals.

―――――>●<―――――

You can't blame the bakers for striking. All they wanted was more dough!

―――――>●<―――――

Women are now honored for their participation in WW II at the Wac's Museum.

―――――>●<―――――

Did you know that retreads were made for people who wanted to retire?

―――――>●<―――――

A woman started a bee farm. She wanted to keep buzzy.

―――――>●<―――――

Shirley Bloom invented the safety pin, in the mid 1800's. The first ones didn't work. But she stuck to it till one did.

There's a school in New Orleans where they graduate girl Santa Clauses. Each student hopes to graduate in the Sister Nickolas class.

——➤●◀——

The first elementary school was a real classy place.

——➤●◀——

The inventor of gum first thought of it on the chew-chew train.

——➤●◀——

Did you know that the first library was started in Booklyn?

——➤●◀——

A diaper manufacturer gave the first New Year's potty.

——➤●◀——

He's a flower child...he can lilac anything.

——➤●◀——

Girl student in pastoral college: "My professors say that if I don't study, I'll be in their class for reverend ever."

——➤●◀——

It was our first day in Russia. Dinner was announced ...Soviet.

——➤●◀——

Svelte: The way your ankles get when they are sprained.

——➤●◀——

How do you tell the sex of a chromosome? You take down its gene.

Susan Simpson is an M.D., an obstetrician. She works in the "Ladies-ready-to-bear" department.

———⇒◄⇐———

A Chicago, Illinois woman was very hard of hearing, then she began to use "mystical" ear ointment and in four days heard from her sister in Springfield.

"Oh, wow! Thanks for the noserings, Grandma."

Don't worry if you have headaches...they're all in your mind!

Our drugstore has a birth-control section. There is a sign above it that reads: "Use the pill; don't make a fetal mistake."

———⟫●⟪———

Maggie Turley's boyfriend is a lawyer and she complained that he'd stayed up all night trying to break her will.

———⟫●⟪———

This guy goes to the doctor complaining that every time he puts his hat on he hears music. The doctor fixed the problem by removing the guy's hat.

———⟫●⟪———

In some art galleries the Venus de Milo is known as "the Goddess of disarmament."

———⟫●⟪———

A pessimist has been defined as one who looks at the world through woes-colored glasses.

———⟫●⟪———

Did you hear about the soprano who couldn't find anyone to sing with. So she went out and bought herself a duet-yourself kit.

———⟫●⟪———

Elmer Tompkin's daughter is shacking up with a guy. Her dad called her boyfriend his sin-in-law.

———⟫●⟪———

Si Bauer was a life-long math teacher...When he died they installed a gravestone that read: "Boy! Have I got problems."

Did you know that Betty Crocker is a flour child?

—————>⊸⊸<—————

One time Chico Marx stormed on the stage floor and shouted at Groucho: "Groucho, you bum. I've got a bone to pick with you!"

"Not with me," said Groucho, "I'm a vegetarian."

—————>⊸⊸<—————

A woman called the local mental hospital and asked if any inmates had escaped in the last couple of days.

"No," replied a nurse, "We've had no escapes at all. Why do you ask?"

"Somebody just ran off with my husband," was the reply. "Some woman who must have been plumb nuts!"

—————>⊸⊸<—————

"How long have you been married, Mrs. Brown?"

"Twenty odd years, Sir, twenty odd years."

"But why do you say twenty <u>odd</u> years?"

"Just wait till you meet my husband."

—————>⊸⊸<—————

"At heart, my wife was immature. I'd be at home, taking a bath and she'd enter the bathroom and sink my boats."

Woody Allen

—————>⊸⊸<—————

There are days when I wake up grouchy. And there are other days when I let him sleep.

—————>⊸⊸<—————

Someone has defined a diplomat as a guy who can convince his wife that a fur coat will make her look fat.

"Tell me the truth about my poor husband, Doctor," said the woman to the physician.

"You must know, Ma'am, that your husband is completely crazy, off his rocker," as they say. "His mind is completely gone."

"I'm not at all surprised, Doctor. You know, he's been giving me a piece of it every derned day for the last twelve years."

———————

"It's a funny thing," said the beautiful girl to her handsome date, "But I couldn't figure out just where my husband was spending his evenings."

"So...what did you do about it?" asked her boyfriend.

"Nothing much. I just went home one night and there he was."

———————

Real women don't have hot flashes. They have power surges.

———————

There are two ways to handle a woman and nobody knows either of them.

Kim Hubbard

———————

Q: Why did God create woman?
A: Because when he took a close look at Adam, he realized he was going to need some help.

———————

Women who think they are the equal of men lack ambition.

This guy was staying every night at the office and his lonesome wife, suspicious, called the office one night but nobody was there. She confronted him about his escapades furiously but he stood up to her, saying, "If you must know, I have been running around every night. And tonight is no different. I'm going out and do you know who is going to shine my shoes, press my suit and pick out my shirt and tie?"

"You bet I do," replied his wife, "The undertaker."

He and I had an office so tiny that an inch smaller and it would have been adultery.

Dorothy Parker

Rita and Polly were having coffee one morning when Rita noticed that Polly looked unwell. "What's the matter, Polly?" she asked.

"Not a lot. It's just that last night I told my boyfriend that I didn't want to see him again!"

"So...what did he say?"

"Not a blamed thing. He just pulled the covers over his head and went to sleep."

"Please tell me, Mrs. Adams, have you other skills worth mentioning for this office?"

"Well, I can tell you this. Last year I had a novel published and sold two short stories to a national magazine."

"But I was considering skills you could apply during office hours."

"Well, those were all done during office hours," she replied.

A sophisticated woman offered this advice to her young, naive friend: "Just remember that a brute is an imperfect animal. Man, and man alone, is a perfect *beast!*"

———>●<———

Elmer was the office bore, constantly bragging about his background and lineage. One day he announced, "All that I am I owe to my mother."

"I have a suggestion," one office worker said to him, "Send her a quarter and square the account."

———>●<———

Why does a woman work ten years to change a man's habits and then complain that he's not the man she married?

Barbra Streisand

———>●<———

When a husband and wife have got each other, the devil only knows which has got the other.

Honore de Balzac (1799-1850)

———>●<———

"Darling, tell me…am I the first man you ever made love with?" the groom asked on their wedding night.

"You certainly are. But why do men always ask that same silly question?"

———>●<———

A famous opera singer once said, "This will give you an idea of what a poor opinion I have of myself, and how little I deserve it."

The Japanese have a word for it. It's judo — the art of conquering by yielding. The Western equivalent of judo is, "Yes, dear."

J.P. McElvoy

"Isn't it a miracle us meeting?
You're everything I've always wanted to change in a man."

Back of every achievement is a proud wife and a surprised mother-in-law.

Brook Hays

A fourth grade girl began her homework project on males this way: "Men are what women marry. They smoke and drink and cuss and don't ever go to church. True, they are a bit more logical than women and more zoological. Both men and women come from monkeys but the women came further than men." Mark Twain had views on the same subject: "I believe that our heavenly father invented men because he was disappointed in monkeys."

———⟫●⟪———

Wedded persons may thus pass over their lives quietly...if the husband becomes deaf and the wife blind.

Richard Taverner

———⟫●⟪———

A good marriage would be between a blind wife and a deaf husband.

Michel de Montaigne
(1533-1592)

———⟫●⟪———

She said he proposed something on their wedding night her own brother wouldn't have suggested.

James Thurber

———⟫●⟪———

A working girl is one who quit her job to get married.

E. J. Kiefer

———⟫●⟪———

Dora and I are now married, but just as happy as we were before.

Bertrand Russell

———⟫●⟪———

All marriages are happy. It's the living together afterward that causes all the trouble.

Raymond Hull

They call her *Checkers*. She jumps when you make a bad move...

———————

When is a young lady like a music box? When she is full of *airs*...

———————

A woman was enjoying her first Caribbean cruise but she was unhappy with seating arrangements at the dinner table. So she went to the captain and said, "Sir, I'm tired of sitting at a table with only women. Couldn't you find some nice, unattached males for us?"

The next evening she came into the dining room to find the captain had done something about her complaint. At her table she was greeted by five smiling priests.

———————

Dinah Shore was once introduced as "the toast of radio," "the toast of movies" and "the toast of television." Her response: "I love the way you buttered that toast!"

———————

At a party, a group was discussing political differences between husbands and wives. A young bride, a Democrat, was asked how she and her Republican husband managed their differences.

She replied: "It's not a problem now because we've been too busy launching a third party."

———————

She calls him *Pilgrim*. Every time he calls he makes a little progress.

———————

A man in a neighboring city calls his wife *Roe*, because she's a little dear.

A certain young man calls his sweetheart *"Silence,"* because when he wants to kiss she gives consent...

———>●●<———

What does a drunken husband's thirst end in? Why, in *bier*...

———>●●<———

At a Wisconsin casino, a woman began to play roulette. She had never gambled before and knew not the first thing about the game. A friend, with her, suggested she play the number representing her age. So, she played number 28. The ball rolled around and finally settled on 38. Immediately, she fainted! Not from the $500 she had bet and lost, but that the number revealed her age.

———>●●<———

This notice appeared in the local paper: "Mrs. Samuel Elder slipped on the ice, fell and hurt her somewhat."

———>●●<———

Why do old maids wear mittens? To keep off the *chaps*...

———>●●<———

If a woman was to change her sex, what religion would she be? *He-then*...

———>●●<———

An usher was passing a collection plate at a famous family wedding. The usher was heard to say: "Yes, ma'am, it is a bit unusual but the father of the bride requested it."

———>●●<———

Why are old maids the most charming of people? Because they are *matchless*.

Why is the world like a mountain? Because it is an *assent*.

———✦———

Two women, old-time friends, were watching a performance of Shakespeare. The one said, "I do wish they'd turn up the lights. I can't hear worth a darn when it's so dark."

Her friend replied: "I feel for you, Honey. I can't hear over the telephone without my glasses."

"Like everybody, Cecil has his faults,
but deep down in his wallet he's really a nice guy."

An unfortunate young man is searching for his sweetheart who was recently carried away by her feelings...

The young woman who was driven to distraction now fears she will have to walk back...

———⟫●⟪———

A woman was shopping in a grocery store and picked up a bottle of olives. She said to her friend: "I always hated these things until I learned how to fix 'em with gin and vermouth."

———⟫●⟪———

The lady who was lost in slumber has found her way out on a nightmare...

———⟫●⟪———

Wanted: Some of the beer produced when mischief is brewing...

———⟫●⟪———

The Sunday School teacher asked her class this: "Can any of you kids tell me the story of Adam and Eve?"

One little girl said, "I can, Teacher."

The teacher nodded to the girl to go ahead and this was her story: "God created Adam first out of the box...Then he looked at Adam and said, 'I can do lots better than that' and created Eve."

———⟫●⟪———

Another Sunday School class had the same question asked of them. When the class was dismissed and the kids were once again home, the father asked the son to tell the story of Adam and Eve. This was the tale: "The teacher told us that God made the first man and woman and then told us how He did it!"

Daddy asked, "Did he really tell you that?"

"He sure did and a little girl took over for the rest of the story. She said, 'God made the guy first. But the guy was very lonely and had nobody to talk to. So, God put the guy to sleep, and while he was snoring, God took out his brains and made a woman of them.'"

———>●<———

The lady that took everybody's eye must have a lot of them...

———>●<———

Why were the Egyptians good sons? Because they paid great respect to their *mummies*.

———>●<———

Paul: "Sir, I want to marry your daughter."
Father: "How much money do you make?"
Paul: "Three hundred bucks a month."
Father: "If you put that with her allowance of $150 a month, that'll make a total of $450."
Paul: "No, Sir, it won't! I've already added that in my figure."

———>●<———

The slick chick from the office came in one morning to announce: "I went out with a real rich guy from Chicago and what do you think he gave me? Five hundred bucks." "Wow!" exclaimed the girl at the next desk. "That's the first time I ever heard of a $475 tip."

———>●<———

Man is: A worm. He comes along, wriggles a bit, and then some chick gets him.

———>●<———

The poor jerk lost his job, lost his car, lost his credit at the bank, but he took his trouble like any man would...he blamed them on his wife.

Man is merely dust, and woman settles him.

Anonymous

———>●<———

My first husband was such an animal that when he went to the zoo, he had to buy two tickets...one to get in and one to get out!

Unknown

———>●<———

On their first date, the young guy insisted that his girl pay half the checks they accumulated during a lovely evening. When they got back to her house, they stood on the porch and the guy started making a pass at the girl.

"Listen, fellow, since we've gone dutch on everything tonight, why don't you just kiss yourself goodnight."

———>●<———

"Mom, I can't marry that young millionaire you've had me going out with the last month. He doesn't believe in hell!"

"Don't let that bother you, Dear," said Mom, "Marry him and we'll change his mind."

———>●<———

A much-divorced woman was asked to give her definition of the difference between lover and husband. "Day and Night," she replied.

———>●<———

Mary: "What's so unusual about your boyfriend?"
Sally: "He chews on his nails."
Mary: "That's not so unusual. Lots of guys chew on their nails."
Sally: "On their *toe* nails?"

———>●<———

Boy: "Cutie, if I only had a nickel for every girl I've kissed..."
Girl: "I know, you'd be able to buy a pack of gum."

Did you hear about the wife who was so concerned about her husband's happiness that she hired two detectives to find out the reason?

———>●<———

Men are nicotine-soaked, beer-besmirched, whiskey greased, red-eyed devils.

Carry Nation (1846-1911)

———>●<———

In the butcher department at the food market, a woman was at the meat counter trying to buy a steak. As the clerk showed it to her, another woman ran up to the counter and said, "I need it quickly, at once, a pound of cat food. Please get it for me now!"

Then she turned to the first woman and said, "I do hope you don't mind my pushing in like this?"

"Not at all," said the first woman. "If you're that hungry, not at all."

"Have you ever considered donating your brain to science? Who knows? Someday a baboon may need a transplant."

Masters Agency

CHAPTER EIGHT

The field of humor is crowded only when Congress is in session.

— Will Rogers

Men are the devil — they all are bearing woe.
In winter it's easy to just say "no."
But what are you going to do in the spring?

Mary Carolyn Davis
A Prayer for Every Day, 1925

———━◗◆◖━———

What is man, when you come to think upon him, but a minutely set, ingenious machine for turning with infinite artfulness the red wine of shiraz into urine.

Isac Dinesen
The Dreamers, 1934

———━◗◆◖━———

A troop of soldiers was resting beside the road when a young girl came down the road leading a donkey.

"Say, little girl," one soldier called out: "You sure are holding that rein awful tight on your brother, aren't you?"

"Yep! I have to," was her reply. "If I didn't he'd surely join the army."

———━◗◆◖━———

Husband: "Dear, everyone I know is talking about the Florsheims and their arguments. Some people take his side and others take the other side."

Wife: "And I suppose some folks are minding their own business!"

————>≈≈<————

Woman to her friend: "I'm looking for that special guy...mature, elderly with a strong will...made out to me."

————>≈≈<————

Old married couple: The wife says to the old man, "When we first married, you always called me Princess, and now...?"
Husband: "Now we have a democracy!"

————>≈≈<————

If you ever had the idea that no two women think alike, you've never been to a pot luck supper!

————>≈≈<————

First wife: "Has your husband lived up to all the promises he made before you were married?"
Second wife: "Just one."
First wife: "Which one was that?"
Second wife: "He said he wasn't good enough for me."

————>≈≈<————

"I just heard that your fiancé is now doing settlement work," one girl said to her friend.
"Yep! That's right. His creditors finally caught up with him."

————>≈≈<————

New wife: "Doctor, you must help me. My husband goes around emptying ash trays. He even does it in public places. I'm about to go nuts."

Psychiatrist: "That's not so unusual. Lots of people go around emptying ash trays."
Wife: "Into their mouths?"

———⟫●⟪———

Farmer husband: "Dear, I think I'll kill a nice fat hen to celebrate our 25th wedding anniversary."
Farmer's wife: "No, dear, don't do that! Why punish a poor chicken for what happened 25 years ago?"

———⟫●⟪———

Son: "Hey, Mom, here's my report card, along with an old one of yours that I found in the attic."
Mom: "Well, Son, this old card of mine isn't any better than yours. I admit it. I guess I'll just have to give you what my Mom gave me!"

———⟫●⟪———

Have you heard the one about the wife of a frequent public speaker who took her husband's temperature with a barometer instead of a thermometer? It read: "dry and windy."

———⟫●⟪———

Wife: "Dear, that's a lovely rainbow tie you're wearing."
Husband: "What do you mean, rainbow tie?"
Wife: "It has a big pot at the end."

———⟫●⟪———

Wife: "How's your secretary, Shirley, these days?"
Husband: "I don't know, I had to fire her."
Wife: "Really. Why?"
Husband: "Well, I just didn't have time, during dictation, to look up all those words I dictated to her."

On the first day of Spring, my dear hubby gave to me: five packs of fertilizer, three packs of seed, two cans of weed killer, a bottle of insect spray and a sharp knife for the pear tree!

———>⊛<———

I've been married about five years and it's about time I had children. I need them while my parents are still young enough to take care of them.

———>⊛<———

This girl was an absolute nut about recycling. She considered it so important that she wouldn't marry a man until he'd been recycled.

———>⊛<———

Rumor has it that men like cars and women like clothes. But don't forget that women, too, like cars mainly because they take them to clothes.

———>⊛<———

"How is the new married life doing for you?" a friend asked the newly-wed guy.

"It's great! My wife is lovely, loyal, meek, great housekeeper and cooks like a great chef. And she's honest and faithful."

"How do you know all this?"

"She told me so herself!"

———>⊛<———

A banker in Denver, Colorado, after reading many surveys on the matter, determined that women controlled most of the nation's wealth. He commented to his partner that it was quite apparent that: "Women not only rock the cradle but cradle all the rocks."

The son of a Protestant father always played with the little Catholic girl next door. One day they got caught in a terrible storm and soaking wet, came to the boy's mother. She took their clothes and put them in warm water in a tub. Warm once again, and dried off, they dressed and the little girl went home. "Mom, now I know, at last," said the little boy, "the difference between a Protestant and a Catholic."

———————

"Aren't you ashamed to let your wife continually browbeat you?" a friend asked the hen-pecked husband.

That evening, the wimp strode into his home and said to his wife: "What time is dinner?" She replied: "Seven-thirty as usual."

"No, Ma'am!" he exclaimed, "You'll serve it at seven sharp. And after supper I want you to put my tuxedo and formal shirt and tie out. I'm taking my blonde secretary dancing."

The wife froze with wonder and then hubby said, "And about my black tie — do you know who is going to tie it?"

The shocked wife finally found her tongue and replied; "I sure do, it's the man from the Eldorado Funeral parlor."

After the above incident, the husband bought a new book "How to be Master in Your Own Home." But he returned it to the clerk, saying, "My wife wouldn't let me keep it."

———————

"My sweetheart," the wife murmured to her husband, "I always tell everybody that you have the face of a saint." But, under her breath she added: "That is...a Saint Bernard."

———————

Sticking her head in the door on a Friday morning, the neighbor woman asked the man's wife, "How is our old friend feeling this morning?"

"He can't complain," his wife assured her.

"Good Golly! I had no idea he was that sick!" was her response.

—————>●<—————

At a party an authoress known for her acerbic tongue, was heard reassuring her "friend": "enjoy yourself while you can, dear. After all, you only live nine lives."

—————>●<—————

A man was worried about his aged mother and hired a psychologist to work with her at the house to see if she was normal for her age. "Be sure you don't let her know that I've hired you for this purpose," the son said.

In the kitchen the psychologist found the old lady cooking a lamb stew and soon had her talking freely. He held up a spoon and asked, "Mama, can you tell me what this is?" "A spoon, for sure," she replied. Then he held up a fork that she readily recognized. Then he held up a knife and asked: "Mama, what is this?"

Mama wrinkled her cheeks, stared at the knife for some time and then asked: "Is it, perhaps, a phallic symbol?"

—————>●<—————

We had a lot in common. I loved him and he loved him.
                              Shelley Winters
                              1952

—————>●<—————

Women have served all these centuries as looking-glasses possessing the magic and delicious power of reflecting the figures of man at twice its natural size.
                              Virginia Woolfe
                              Room of One's Own,
                              1929

"That was the interior decorator. He says you'll have to go!"

For the first year of marriage I had a basically bad attitude. I tended to place my wife underneath a pedestal.

Woody Allen

———

It is possible that blondes also prefer gentlemen.

Mamie Van Doren

———

He is every other inch a gentleman.

Rebecca West
(1892-1983)

A man is as young as the woman he feels.

Unknown

———⟫●⟪———

I believe that sex is the most beautiful, natural and whole-some thing that money can buy.

Steve Martin

———⟫●⟪———

When a rogue kisses you, count your teeth.

Hebrew Proverb

———⟫●⟪———

I regard men as a pleasant pastime but no more dependable than the British weather.

Anne Raeburn
British Therapist BBC-TL
1990

———⟫●⟪———

Grow your own dope...plant a man.

———⟫●⟪———

A girl walked into the restaurant and ordered eggs.
"How would you like your eggs cooked?" asked the waitress.
The girls answered: "Hey, that'll be just great!"

———⟫●⟪———

Young woman: "I want to buy a diamond ring."
Salesman: "Certainly, Ma'am. Would you like one of our combination sets? They are of three pieces; engagement, wedding, and teething."

A woman walked into a fancy dress shop and told the manager: "I'm the best damned salesgirl in this whole state and I want a job."

The manager replied: "That's quite a commendation but I don't have any openings."

Unfazed, the woman asks: "How many dresses does your top salesgirl sell in a day?"

"Five or six," said the manager.

"I'll sell a dozen just to prove how good I am," said the applicant.

Knowing she couldn't lose, the manager agreed. So, the new girl started to work. And before closing she'd sold nineteen dresses. "Do I get the job now?" she demanded.

"I've got one more test for you," said the manager. He went to the back of the store and returned with the most hideous dress ever seen, saying, "Sell this dress before store closing and you've got a job."

Just before the closing bell sounded, the girl walked into the manager's office and gave him the sales receipt. "I'm simply amazed," the manager said. "How on earth did you convince anyone to buy that awful rag?"

"Getting her to buy it was easy," said the girl. "The tough part was strangling her seeing-eye dog."

If no man ever said anything unless he knew what he was talking about, a ghastly hush would descend upon the earth.

Dalan Herbert

It's better to keep one's mouth shut and be thought a fool than to open it and resolve all doubt.

Generally speaking I look upon sports as dangerous and tiring activities performed by people with whom I share nothing except the right of trial by jury.

Fran Lebowitz

Did you hear about the husband who heard that it costs only ten dollars a year to support a kid in India? So, he sent his kid there.

———⟫◦⟪———

Is that guy stupid? Well, I guess! He recently studied for a full week before he took a urine test.

-DLETCH-

Dumb Men Jokes

Did you hear about Martin Jenkins who was given just two weeks to live? He decided to take one week in June and the other in January.

Emil Jenkins said the best ten years of his life had been spent in third grade.

—————⊃⊃●《⊂—————

Did you hear about Al Jones? He was walking down the street when he met his friend Florin with a sack over his shoulder. "What have you got in the sack, Florin?" Al asked.

"Chickens," Florin replied. "And if you can guess how many I've got I'll give you both of them."

Al answered: "Three!"

—————⊃⊃●《⊂—————

Charlie Peters approached the Navy department with a great idea for the Navy to be used in future wars. It was an invention of screen windows to keep the fish out of submarines.

—————⊃⊃●《⊂—————

Two guys stored their fishing boat at the dock and one asked: "Did you mark the place where we caught all the fish?"

"Sure did. I marked it right on the side of the boat."

"Yeah, but what if they give us another boat the next time we go fishin'?"

—————⊃⊃●《⊂—————

That same guy who marked the boat to find where the fishin' was good, the next time he and his buddy went out, entered the boat with his friend and half way to where they wanted to go, a hole in the front of the boat let water steadily into the boat. So he drilled a hole in the other end to let the water out!

—————⊃⊃●《⊂—————

How do you burn a dumb guy's ear? Call him up while he's ironing. Yeah, but what about his other ear? Have him call the doctor.

Did you hear about the terrorist, Edward Tall? He was sent to Chicago to bomb a bus in front of the Wrigley Building and burnt his lips on the exhaust pipe.

The podiatrist examined the man's feet and advised him to put a clean pair of socks on every day. The problem was that by the end of the week, the guy couldn't get his shoes on.

Q: Why do men only get a half hour for lunch?
A: So the boss won't have to retrain them.

Tom had formed a dance band and they had a new job at the American Legion Building. Tom was real pleased with the gig and, after they were well into the playing, he asked the trombonist: "Pete, go outside and see what it sounds like, will ya?"
Pretty soon, Pete came back and said: "It sounds terrific. You ought to hear it!"
So the whole band went out to listen.

Four Arkansas men were having a few too many drinks when they decided to take a walk. They started out and soon came to a brick wall. "What's on the other side?" one of them asked. "Boost me on yore shoulder an' ah'll tell ya," one of the guys said. So they boosted him upon their shoulders and he yelled down, "It's a nudist camp."
"Men or women?" they asked.
"Can't tell. They ain't got no clothes on!"

A husband is a guy who wishes he had as much fun on his night out as his wife thinks he does.

Anonymous

"My husband would like to see that fur coat you showed me yesterday."

Q: What do you call a man with his hands handcuffed behind his back?
A: Trustworthy.

———

Q: Why do men have clean consciences?
A: Because they never use them.

———

Q: Why is psychoanalysis a lot quicker for men than women?
A: Because when it's time to go back to childhood, most men are already there.

———

It is funny the two things men are proudest of is the thing that any man can do and does in the same way, that is being drunk and being the father of their son.

Gertrude Stein
(1874-1946)

Q: What do men consider a seven-course dinner?
A: A six pack and a hamburger.

Q: What do you call an intelligent man in America?
A: A tourist.

. A newlywed was talking to her mother about her marriage. "Mom, it really is an awful grind. I never could have believed it could be like this."

"What do you mean, Daughter?" Mom asked.

"I have to wash dishes, make the beds, tidy up the living room, mop the floors and then two weeks later I have to do it all over again."

Spring: The season when a boy begins to think about what the girls have been thinking about all winter.

Stalemate: A husband who is beginning to smell musty.

Two teachers were chatting about their students. "Kids sure are funny," one said. "You know, they give each other nicknames. One boy in my class is named 'Will Knot' and they call him 'Won't.'

The other teacher said, "And I have a boy named 'Nosmo King.' The other kids call him 'No Smoking.'"

Hubby: "Dear, can you think of something that'll put a finishing touch on my short story?"
Wife: "Yes. A match."

The first grade teacher was having a "show and tell" session with her class. The kids were to talk about their fathers. One little girl said that her father was a lawyer. Another said hers was a plumber, and a little boy said his father worked in a department store.

"So, tell us, Alice, what does your father do?"

"He watches lots of football and baseball games on television," Alice said, "but his main job is to take out the garbage."

———⟫●⟪———

Husband: "Honey, you need more exercise. Why not try touching your toes to loosen your muscles?"
Wife: "Let me tell you something! If God wanted me to touch my toes He'd have put them on my knees!"

———⟫●⟪———

"Doctor, my wife is pregnant and now is having contractions four minutes apart!"

"Just take it easy, Sir," advised the physician on the other end of the line. "Is this her first child?"

"Hell no!" shouted the husband, "This is her husband!"

———⟫●⟪———

Judy: "Tom, I wish I had a lower IQ so I could enjoy your company."

———⟫●⟪———

The hospital surgeon was making the rounds to treat his patients and stopped in to see a young woman on whom he had operated a few days before.

"Doctor, will the scar left on me show?" she asked.

"That's altogether up to you, Miss," he replied.

The little boy asked his mother: "Momma, did you see the stork that brought me?"

"Only the bill, son, only the bill!" was mommy's reply.

———⟫•⟪———

"Can you tell me why my sweetie always closes her eyes when I kiss her?"

"Take a look in the mirror and you'll know."

———⟫•⟪———

"Do you have the book, *Man, Master of Women*?" the young man asked the librarian.

"The fiction section is second to your left," she replied.

———⟫•⟪———

Boy: "Do you think you could find happiness with a guy like me?"

Girl: "Probably, if he isn't too much like you."

———⟫•⟪———

A woman's aunt, almost 90, was taken suddenly to a rest home for a two-week trial visit. When her daughter took her there, she packed a small overnight bag with the rest of her necessities.

Two days later, her daughter got a phone call from mother telling her to "Please bring more clothes. Bring that new pink print dress and my floral blouse and do bring my sequined cocktail dress. And bring all my cosmetics. You didn't tell me they had men here."

———⟫•⟪———

Daughter: "Mom, look at this lovely engagement ring, isn't it lovely?"

Mother: "It's something, all right. I'd rather you'd married a boy with money."

Boy: "Sally, don't you think I'm rather good looking?"
Girl: "In a way."
Boy: "What kind of way?"
Girl: "Way off!"

———>○<———

Girl to boyfriend: "Look, Charlie, I'm not going to engage in a war of wits with you. I never fight with an unarmed man."

———>○<———

"Yesterday a burglar broke into our home."
"Did he get anything?"
"I'll say! My wife thought I was coming home late."

———>○<———

A bum stopped a man on the street and asked for a dime for a cup of coffee. The man said, "I'll give you the dime on one condition...that you take me with you to get the cup of coffee. I want to see the place they still sell coffee for a dime!"

———>○<———

It was a large cocktail party and several hundred guests milled about drinking, eating hors d'oeuvres, talking and having a good time. Suddenly a woman came up to the hostess and said, "Pardon me, but can you help me find that pretty little blonde girl who was passing out drinks a short time ago?"
"What is it you want...a drink?"
"Nope. I'm looking for my husband."

———>○<———

A car was speeding down the highway when a flying patrolman spotted her. He radioed his partner on the ground and that policeman stopped the woman and began to write a citation. "But how in the world did you know I was speeding?" she asked.

The patrolman said nothing, merely pointed skyward.

"Are you telling me that *He's* against me, too?" she groaned.

———⟫●⟪———

It is the easiest thing in the world to say "Every broad for herself," and saying it and acting that way is one thing that's kept some of us behind the eight ball where we've been living for a hundred years.

> Billie Holliday

———⟫●⟪———

Two women, old friends, met on the street one day and began to ask one another how the summer had gone. "Did you do anything to the house over the summer?" one woman asked the other.

"You bet I did; I always improve the house during the summer, what with remodeling and all. But this year I did something special to make things nicer at home. I got rid of my husband."

———⟫●⟪———

In evolutionary terms, females are more advanced than males. Women are more human than men.

> Ashley Montague and M. Roy
> *The Natural Superiority of Women,*
> 1952

———⟫●⟪———

Fathers should be neither seen nor heard. That is the only basis for family life.

> Oscar Wilde

Daddy was giving Bible lessons to his kids and asked, "Why was King Solomon the wisest man in the world?"

His wife answered him: "Because he had so many wives giving him advice."

———>•‹———

Her husband had just passed away and been taken to the funeral parlor when she got a call: "Madam, we're confused. We don't know whether instructions were to bury your husband or cremate him. What shall we do?"

"Take no chances," she replied. "Do both."

———>•‹———

"How can you stop a husband from drowning?"
"First thing...take your foot off his head!"

———>•‹———

"I've just buried my second husband," said the woman to her friend. "I'll never marry again."

"What happened that you lost two husbands?" the friend asked.

"The first husband died from eating poison mushrooms," was the reply.

"And what happened to the second husband?"
"He was shot to death."
"Really! How come?"
"He wouldn't eat the mushrooms."

———>•‹———

Have you heard about the new eyeglass invented for men to watch girls in mini-skirts?

It's called thigh-focals.

"We've been married thirty years," Eddie said to his buddies who were in his house for the weekly poker game. "And she still corrects me every time I open my mouth."

"31 years," his wife called out from the kitchen.

———>●<———

Susie, the daughter of the house, had come to her mother to get marital advice. "You'd best talk to your father," she advised her daughter. "He made a much better marriage decision than I did."

———>●<———

The husband had been giving his wife holy hell for several hours. Finally she said, "You may not have had a happy childhood, but you sure had a long one."

———>●<———

"Honey," hubby said to his wife, "It does seem that you lie a little now and then."

"I do," she admitted, "but I think a wife has the inherent duty to say good things about her husband, now and then."

———>●<———

"It's a queer thing, dear," Tom said to his wife, "but after I shave of a morning, I feel ten years younger."

"That gives me an idea," his wife replied. "Why don't you shave yourself before you go to bed at night?"

———>●<———

"I must tell you, Mrs. Jones, that I cannot cure your husband of talking in his sleep."

"You misunderstand me, Doctor. I don't want you to cure him of talking in his sleep. What I want you to do is make him talk more clearly."

"Mamie, I heard your husband, Peter, is in the hospital. What on earth is wrong with him?"

"It's just his knee that's involved. I caught a blonde on it."

———>●<———

If love makes the world go 'round, why are we going to outer space?

———>●<———

Sometimes you can't help but worry about what the world is turning into. Consider my son's teacher who moonlights as a cab driver. The neighborhood cop has a part-time job at a bowling alley. Almost all folks are holding down two jobs. In all humanitarian history, no group of people has worked as hard as this present one to acquire all the latest labor-saving appliances.

"You broke a hundred? So did I!"

"I hate to say this Sweetheart, but this toast is terribly tough," the husband said to his wife.

"The trouble is, Dear, that you're eating the paper plate."

Elmer completed his bath, then said to his wife, "Do you think the neighbors would say anything if I mowed the grass in the nude?"

"They might say that I married you for your money."

Q: What do you get when you cross a federal income tax officer with a rose?

A: A blooming idiot.

The stock market craze has just about everybody investing. This one guy was asked by his sweet wife whether he'd been a bull or a bear in the market that day. He replied like this: "I've been neither of them. I've been a jackass, that's what!"

"Dad," the boy asked his father, "What is a millennium?"

"Son, I think it's a centennial but with a lot more legs."

Mabel's husband is so dumb. He almost had a nervous breakdown trying to decide which part of an olive to throw away.

Marriage is an alliance between two people, one of whom never remembers birthdays, and the other who never forgets them.

Mabel was a freshman in college when she arrived home one Thanksgiving vacation. "Mama," she said to Mom, "I just got to tell you. I'm going to have a baby."

Mom responded like this: "Promise me you won't tell your father. With his bad heart, this just might kill him."

"I won't tell him, Mom," was the reply.

"And don't tell your brother. With his big mouth the whole town will know about it before nightfall."

"Just as you say, Mom...but what about you? Aren't you going to say something to me?"

"Not a word. I don't want to make a scene. I'll just go upstairs now to my room and commit suicide."

———➤●◄———

Paul's wife refused to allow the nurse to insert in her husband a rectal thermometer. "Why do you resist that, Ma'am?" the nurse asked.

"Because you'll damage his brain," was the wife's reply.

———➤●◄———

Finally Pauline refused to take her husband grocery shopping with her. "Why do you do that?" a friend asked.

"Because the lummox always stood in front of the cereal department and saluted the General Mills items."

———➤●◄———

Tommy and Martha were having their usual argument at the dinner table. "You're just a dumb bunny," shouted Tommy.

"That's just not so," Martha replied. "My father invented the toilet seat."

"So what?" Tommy yelled back. "My father put the hole in it."

———➤●◄———

When they had returned from their European trip, the secretary at his office asked him about France. "And what did you like best about your trip to Paris?" she asked.

"I just loved hearing those French pheasants sing the Mayonnaise," was his reply.

———>•<———

Two ladies were walking home from church on Sunday when one of them said: "Suzanne, what do you consider your very worst sin?"

Suzanne replied: "I'd have to say vanity, I guess. I just sit in front of my bureau mirror hour after hour admiring my loveliness."

"That shouldn't bother you too much because it's not vanity. It's just imagination."

———>•<———

A welfare worker was interviewing a woman who had asked for welfare.

"Your application says that you have six children, Ma'am. How old is the youngest?"

"He's six months old," was her reply.

"But your application tells me that your husband has been dead for five years. How do you explain that?"

"Sir, it's true that he died five years ago. But I didn't."

———>•<———

The man started across the street when the light turned green, but jumped back to avoid being hit by a woman with a station wagon full of kids.

"Ya dern fool," the guy hollered, "Don't ya know when to stop?"

The lady looked back at the rear seat full of kids and then said, "Sir, they're not *all* mine."

———>•<———

The new secretary was annoyed that nobody in the office noticed her new ring. So she declared in a very loud voice: "Goodness me, it's warm in here! I think I'll take off my ring."

———⟫●⟪———

There's only one thing that can separate the men from the boys: Women!

———⟫●⟪———

"Sweetheart," said the wife to her cheapskate husband, "Is it true that money talks?"

"That's what they say, Honey."

"If that's so, as you say, leave me 50 bucks. I get lonely and need to talk while you're away."

———⟫●⟪———

Q: What is the average man's idea of helping with the housework?

A: Lifting his legs so his wife can finish with the vacuum cleaner.

———⟫●⟪———

A man's life consists of 20 years of having his mother ask him where he's going, 35 years of having his wife ask the same question, and at the end, having the mourners ask the same thing.

———⟫●⟪———

Q: How many men are needed to change a roll of toilet paper?

A: Nobody knows because it hasn't happened yet.

———⟫●⟪———

"Have you heard about the recent book titled *What Men Know About Women*?" asked Jane.

""No," her friend replied, "But I'm going to look for it this afternoon. What's the title again?"

"Never mind the title…just look for the thinnest book in the bookstore."

———⇒●⇐———

Sally's teenage daughter came home from Sunday School to ask her mother: "Mom, why did the Israelites have to wander in the desert forty years when they escaped from Egypt?"

"Because, dear, as far back as then, guys wouldn't stop to ask directions."

———⇒●⇐———

This young woman went to the doctor and asked him how much it would cost to get a brain transplant. The doctor replied: "Well, we have this excellent brain from a young man that costs $40,000."

When the woman complained that she couldn't afford such an expensive organ and asked for something less expensive, the doctor replied: "Well, we do have this one brain that you can get for $15,000.

"But why the difference?" the patient asked.

"Because the cheaper brain is a woman's. It has been used."

———⇒●⇐———

Clarence's wife was getting mighty sick of working with a faulty toilet. "Clarence, the toilet needs repairing," she told him, "And you'll feel much better after you do it."

"What do you mean by that?" Clarence asked.

"Because I'm going to keep awakening you until you do!"

———⇒●⇐———

Tired of that contented look on your husband's face? Try giving him a dish towel.

A woman executive had been having chest pains and went to a cardiologist who gave her a cardiogram, then sent her home. When the woman came back for her next appointment, she asked the doctor, "Was it bad? What did my electro-cardiogram show?"

"Well, let me put it this way. If I put the tape on a player piano, the tune would likely be, 'Nearer My God to Thee.'"

———➤●◀———

An archeologist decided to spend some time at the local bars instead of doing his normal, constant research. So he went to a bar and there met a lovely blonde young lady. They had a few drinks together, then went out to dinner where he asked her to spend the night with him in his apartment. She agreed, and after dinner they took a cab to his apartment where he began to show her some of his archeological relics. Looking at one strange relic, she asked what it was and he told her, "Dear, in some tribes, they worship a phallic symbol and that's what it looks like to me."

"Really!" she replied. "But I'd sure hate to tell you what it looks like to me."

———➤●◀———

"I think it's awful the way women talk today," a well-known playboy told his talk show host. "They really aren't ladies when they use all those four-letter words."

"Like what?" the host asked.

"Like can't and won't and don't."

———➤●◀———

Husband to exhausted wife: "Honey, do you believe in free love?"

"Have I ever sent you a bill?" she asked.

———➤●◀———

The nice little car slowed to a stop on a deserted country road.

"Sure sorry, Sweetheart," said the young driver with a grin. "I guess we're out of gas."

His beautiful companion said, "Interesting, I was afraid something like this would happen." And she pulled a flask from her pocket book.

"You surprise me," said the guy. "What did you bring — scotch, bourbon or rye?"

"Gasoline," she replied.

"I rate you a ten, Fenton — but that's on a scale of one to a hundred."

The guy and his wife were having a furious argument about his golf game and his constant absence out playing golf.

"Oh, be quiet!" he demanded, "You're driving me out of my mind."

"That wouldn't be a drive...that's only a putt," she snapped back.

———————

"I'm going to fire the new laundress...she's been stealing my clothes."

"What did she steal?" her husband asked.

"Those very same towels we got from the hotel in Hot Springs," replied his wife.

———————

"Connie, why did Mary and Joseph take Jesus with them to Jerusalem?"

"I guess because they couldn't find a baby sitter," was her reply.

———————

Ann, a very upset young woman, came into the psychiatrist's office and said: "Doctor, I need help. I love him and he loves me. We like all the same things, books, movies, sports. When away from one another we're miserable. I just don't know what to do!"

"I don't understand, Ma'am," said the psychiatrist. "You love each other, are compatible in all ways, what's the problem?"

"Just this Doctor...what shall I tell my husband!"

———————

"I'm not a rich man, don't own a yacht, don't have any cars like Bobby Edwards, but I love you dearly."

"I love you, too, but tell me more about Bobby Edwards."

———————

A ravishing, talented young woman who had won many beauty contests finally accepted one of her many marriage proposals and, when asked how it felt to be engaged to be married, she replied: "I feel just like a successful business man who's built up his business then finds himself about to go into the hands of the receiver!"

———————

Did you ever wonder and speculate as to why it is so quiet on New Year's Day?

The reason is simply that so many wives aren't speaking to their husbands.

———————

The couple had just been married and as they drove up to the hotel for their first night, the bride said, "Dear, try to act like we've been married for many years...let's not look like newlyweds."

"OK by me," said the groom. "But do you think you can carry all four suitcases?"

———————

A woman called a psychiatrist and said, "Oh, Doctor, you've got to help me. My husband thinks he's Moses, simply insists that he's Moses."

"That does sound serious," replied the psychiatrist. "Do bring him to my office tomorrow."

"Oh, I will. But tell me, Doctor, in the meantime, how do I keep him from parting the water every time I try to take a bath?"

———————

An elderly diva with the Met was trying to impress a much younger singer. "I want you to know that my voice is insured for a hundred thousand dollars."

"Really! Is that so," murmured the younger singer. "Whatever did you do with all that money?"

A little girl went to a big department store, to the perfume counter and said to the salesman: "I want to buy a bit of perfume."

"Here is our newest," said the salesman, "It's called 'A Night of Lust.' Would you like to try it?"

"No," replied the child. "That doesn't seem to fit me. What else do you have?"

"Well, how about 'Flaming Desire'?"

"Nope, Don't think so."

"Here's one more, Miss. It's 'Burning Kiss of Venus'."

"Tell me, Mister, haven't you something for beginners?"

———⟫●⟪———

A beautiful, red sports car roared to a stop at a bus stop and the driver said to the pretty girl waiting there, "I'm going South, Miss Beautiful."

"Oh, great," replied the girl. "Please bring me a grape-fruit."

———⟫●⟪———

There's an ancient expression that has it that 'Two's company, three's a crowd.' But nowadays, a company of two often results in there being three.

———⟫●⟪———

Two old friends were discussing a mutual acquaintance. "I certainly do think that Selma is very kind to her inferiors."

"I agree," said her friend, "considering all the time it took to find them."

"Women think about a lot more than Just clothes and relationships... We're plotting to take over the world, too, or didn't you know?"

CHAPTER NINE

The most comic things of all are the things that are most worth doing — like making love.
                                                — Chesterton

Q: What is it that a woman has two of and a cow has four of?
A: Feet.

—————————>>●<<—————————

"If you happened to catch your canary in your lawnmower, how would you catalog the result?"
"I'd call it shredded tweet."

—————————>>●<<—————————

A woman ran up to a man coming out of a church and asked him: "Is mass out?"
He replied: "No, but your hat's not on straight."

—————————>>●<<—————————

He: "Would you commit adultery for a million dollars?"
She: "Just might. Why?"
He" "Well, then, how about two dollars?"
She: "We've already settled that. Now what about the price!"

—————————>>●<<—————————

"Commiserate with me, Mary, I'm a pauper."
"Really! Is it a boy or a girl?"

There's a most unusual slant to that marriage. They had nothing in common but they kept fooling around until they did.

———⟫●⟪———

Did you ever wonder why so many women cry at weddings? I used to. Then I began to take a closer look at some of the grooms.

———⟫●⟪———

The daughter said to her mother: "Y'know Mom, I went to the Senior ball last night and it was a costume affair. I saw Johnny there but I couldn't tell him from Adam!"

"For goodness sakes, Dear, are you telling me he dressed like that?"

———⟫●⟪———

A guy went into a barber shop to get a shave and a manicure. The manicurist was real cute and he said to her, "Hey, Baby, how about a date with me tonight?"

"Impossible," she said, "You see I'm married."

"Don't let that stop us. Just phone him and tell him you have to work tonight."

"Why don't you tell him. He's shaving you now."

———⟫●⟪———

"Grandma, why do you read the Bible so much?" the little boy asked.

"Well, Eddie, I need to cram for my final examination."

———⟫●⟪———

"That's a beautiful mink coat you're wearing, Mabel," her friend said to the chorus girl. "Is it yours?"

"You're derned tootin' it is," was the reply. "But I'm still making nightly payments on it."

An older man and his wife had three daughters. One of them married a man from Twin Cities, Minnesota and they moved there. In time, the daughter gave birth to twins. Not too long after that, the second girl married and she and her husband moved to Three Rivers, Ontario. Sure enough, soon she gave birth to triplets. Then the youngest sister got engaged and after a long period still did not announce her wedding date, so the father asked her why she was delaying this most important event in her life.

"Well, Daddy," she said, "I must tell you that my future husband wants me to move after we're married to the Thousand Islands and that makes me delay things. Understand?"

Daddy nodded his head, "Yes."

———⟫●⟪———

"Tell me, Jonah, do you like smart women?"

"Let's put it this way," he replied, "I love a girl with a good head on my shoulder."

———⟫●⟪———

Before marriage a man yearns for a woman. After marriage, you drop the "y."

———⟫●⟪———

"I arranged for their marriage."
"You mean you had the shotgun?"

———⟫●⟪———

That ballerina is so fat she has to wear a three-three!
Pun-American Newsletter

———⟫●⟪———

An elderly, retired physician took his wife to a restaurant. He was known all over town as the community's worst cheapskate. At the restaurant they ordered just one ham sandwich that they divided between them. The waiter, knowing the guy, stopped by noticing that the doctor wasn't eating his half-sandwich. "Something wrong with your big, big sandwich, Doctor?" the waiter asked.

"Nope. Everything's fine. It's just that she's using our teeth."

The nurse brought the father his new-born baby and said, "It looks just like you, Sir!"

The Father recited a poem for her:
You say the baby looks like me,
    How sad, I surely dread it!
But the only likeness I can see
    Is that we're both bald-headed.

Boys faithfully imitate their fathers in spite of all efforts to teach them good manners.

Seven-year-old Sally approached her Mother and said, "Mommy, Tommy, the little boy next door wants to get married. Is that OK with you?"

"But Sally," her Mom replied, thinking to have some fun: "How do you expect to live without money?"

"Well, Mommy, I get fifty cents a week and Bobby gets seventy-five. We think that'll do."

"But, Sally, suppose you and Bobby have a baby. What then?"

"Well, so far we've been lucky," Sally replied.

"Tell me, Gladys, why did your boyfriend return his necktie?"

Gladys: "He said it fit him too tight!"

I never know what to get my father for his birthday. I said, "Buy yourself something that will make your life easier." So, he went out and bought a present for my mother.

Rita Rudner

————>●<————

"You have the reputation for being the smartest guy in town. So, tell me...why did God create man?"
"He couldn't teach the women to take out the garbage."

————>●<————

A kind and thoughtful husband presented his wife with a brand new skunk fur coat for their anniversary.
"I just don't understand how it is that such a lovely coat came from such a smelly animal."
The husband blushed and said, "You don't have to say thank you, but you could show me a little respect!"

————>●<————

Did you hear about the dumb guy, a genuine jerk, who got caught in a revolving door for four hours because he couldn't figure out whether he was entering or leaving.

————>●<————

Father: "Dear, don't you think our son gets all of his brains from me?"
Mother: "I do believe so, dear. I still have all of mine."

————>●<————

"Did you hear that young Flanaigan is getting a Ph.D.?"
"What does that mean, a Ph.D.?"
"For him it means poop-headed dope."

A woman entered the cemetery office and said, "I can't locate my husband's grave and yet I know he's buried here."

"What's his name?" the attendant asked.

"Paul Appel," was her reply.

The attendant looked through his file and said, "I can't find a Paul. But we do have a Sally Appel."

"That's it," replied the woman, "Everything is in my name."

———⟶⦁⟵———

Did you hear about the guy who was a very high-up executive? He thought that Herz Van Rentals was a famous Dutch painter.

———⟶⦁⟵———

Q: Why do men have no trouble at all spelling Otto?
A: Probably because there are only two letters to remember.

———⟶⦁⟵———

"Did anyone in your family ever make a brilliant marriage?"

"Yeah. My husband did."

———⟶⦁⟵———

Heading the list of husbands who try us
Are husbands who insistently sleep on the bias.

———⟶⦁⟵———

An attractive, wise old Quaker woman was asked by a member of her meeting: "Penelope, how is it that thee has never married?"

The lady smiled at the question and replied: "As thee knows, it takes a might fine husband to be better than none at all."

310

Two women were having a drink at the bar. One said, "For twenty years my hubby and I were wonderfully happy."

"Then what happened?" someone asked.

"We met," was the reply.

―――⇒●⇐――

Two guys were discussing a friend's marital infidelities. "How on earth does he get away with it? The only thing I've ever done behind my wife's back is to zip her up."

―――⇒●⇐――

An eighty-year-old woman wrote a friend this letter: "I've become a little older since I last saw you, and a few changes have entered my life. I'm seeing five guys a day now. As soon as I wake up of a morning, Will Power helps me get out of bed. Then I go see John. Soon Charlie Horse enters the picture and that takes up a good part of the day. When he leaves, Arthur Itis enters the room and finishes out the day. He doesn't like to stay in one place so he drags me from one joint to another. After all that hectic a day, I hit the hay with Ben Gay. I'm a very busy girl."

―――⇒●⇐――

Irate IRS agent: "What the heck is all this stuff you brought me?"

Taxpayer: "Well, you told me to bring all my records and so you've got 'em."

"Garth Brooks, Dolly Parton and Willie Nelson?"

―――⇒●⇐――

Eddie Parsons was standing in the middle of the hotel lobby without a stitch of clothing on him.

A policeman grabbed him and said, "I'll get a few rags to cover you and then we're going to the police station."

Eddie protested vehemently and the cop said, "You can't go around the lobby stark naked like that."

"But officer, I was awaitin' mah girl friend. She done tol' me to git undressed and we'd go to town. She ain't down-stairs yit."

"If you're fishing for a compliment, you're using the wrong bait!"

The psychiatrist told Debbie that she'd have to be honest with him if he was to be able to help her. She nodded agreement. "So, tell me, Debbie, have you ever looked in your husband's face while making love?"

"Yes."

"Thank you. Now when you looked in his face, what emotion did you see there?"

"Lotsa anger."

"And when you saw this great anger, what was your hus-band doing at the time?"

"He was on a step-ladder, looking at me through the bedroom window."

———⟫◆⟪———

The man with the bulging shopping bag slipped into his seat at the movies just after it began. Once there, he began to search through the bag for some certain item.

One by one he took packages from the bag, opened them and rustled through them, crackling the paper.

Finally, a woman in front of him turned around and hissed this at him: "What are you doing back there...building a nest?"

———⟫●⟪———

"I plumb hate my husband's nasty nature," cried the young bride. "Why he's got me so nervous I'm losing weight."

"Then why don't you up and leave him?" asked her friend.

"I will...bet on it," the bride assured her friend. "I'm just hanging in there until he fetches me down to 125 pounds."

———⟫●⟪———

The single girl, never married, walked into the office one day and passed out cigars and candy, both having blue ribbons tied on them. The office folks were puzzled until she stood in the middle of the floor, held up her hand displaying a solitaire on her left finger and said, "It's a boy — six feet tall and 183 pounds."

———⟫●⟪———

Q: What are the worst six years in the life of an Arkansas man?

A: Fourth grade.

———⟫●⟪———

Emil was a few loads short of a full one when one night he was going home and it was very dark. He ran into a tree, staggered back, then moved ahead and rammed into another tree. This happened two more times. Then he said: "How awful. I was supposed to be home an hour ago and here I am lost in the forest!"

———>∘<———

"Doggone it, Mr. Elwood, you got to quit urinating in our swimming pool!" the lifeguard demanded.
"But almost everybody urinates in this pool," he argued.
"From the diving board?"

———>∘<———

I felt real good about being given a seat of honor by my university. But I'd have felt a lot better if they'd removed the strip that read: "Sanitized For Your Protection."

———>∘<———

Over supper one night, Sally's husband said to her: "All my life I wanted to be someone. I see now I should have been more specific."

———>∘<———

Many a woman wishes she were strong enough to tear a telephone book in half. Especially if she has a teenage daughter.

Guy Lombardo

———>∘<———

There are times when I have to quit thinking...and the only way I can quit thinking is by shopping.

Tammy Faye Baker

During the Depression, she'd get on the bus and present the driver with a day-old transfer. The driver would tell her: "Lady, this transfer is a day too old." And then she'd tell him: "Now you see how long I've been waiting for the bus."

———>•<———

A guy walks up to the desk at the hotel and it's late at night. He's very tired but he sees a very cute blonde in the lobby and goes up to talk to her. He comes back to the desk with her on his arm and says, "I'll need a double room for tonight."

The next morning he goes up to the desk to pay his bill and the clerk presents it to him: It lists his cost at two thousand dollars. "What the hell is this all about?" he screams. "I was only here for one night!"

"Yes, we know," the clerk replied, "but your wife has been here for three weeks."

———>•<———

Most women have had a certain type of night when their hair looked too good to stay home.

———>•<———

The guy says to his hair stylist: "My hair is coming out like crazy. What can I use to keep it in?"

The stylist replied: "How about a shoe box!"

———>•<———

Husband: "If I died would you remarry?"
Wife: "After several months of grieving, I guess I would."
Husband: "Would he live in this house?"
Wife: "It's a lovely, expensive house, so I guess he would."
Husband: "And would he sleep in our bed?"
Wife: "It's a brand new bed, so I guess he would."
Husband: "And if you remarried and slept in this house and in our bed, would he use my golf clubs?"
Wife: "Nope, he's left-handed."

A woman's husband described her husband's concern for her this way: "He's very considerate...he holds the door while I take out the garbage."

———⟫●⟪———

Genevieve's husband was always accusing her of nagging him. One time she replied in this way: "Dear, I don't nag. I motivate."

———⟫●⟪———

Husband: "I'm getting tired of you always saying I'm wrong. Just this once, I'll admit I'm wrong if you'll admit I'm right."
Wife: "You start things."
Hubby: "I'm wrong."
Wife: "You're right."

———⟫●⟪———

"There seems to be no solution to that worldly population explosion," said a woman to her friend.
"Why do you say that?" the friend asked.
"Because there is simply too much fun in lighting the fuse," was her reply.

———⟫●⟪———

The young boy knocked on the door of the neighbor's house and when it opened, he asked, "Can I see your trap?"
"What trap? Whatever are you talking about?" the neighbor asked.
The boy replied, "You know...the one my Dad says you can't keep shut."

———⟫●⟪———

Mrs. Golly gave generous Christmas checks to her grandchildren every Christmas. But the kids never bothered to thank her. Then, one Christmas things changed.

Grandma sent generous checks to the kids and the very next day the kids came over to thank her. A friend asked: "What do you think caused them to be suddenly so thoughtful?"

"Simple," grandma replied. "This year I didn't sign the checks!"

———⟫●⟪———

Today more fathers are helping with the baby than ever before. But it's often hard for guys who have no previous experience. Mrs. Elmer Jones solved the problem in her home in this way. "John, please diaper the baby. How? This way: consider the diaper a baseball diamond, bring second base to home plate and lay the baby between first and third. Now bring first, third and home together and pin. And, be sure to dust home plate with a bit of talcum powder. Pretty much a stroke of genius, right?"

———⟫●⟪———

"What kind of game did you have in mind?" the girl asked.

"What about Post Office?" he replied.

"Post Office? That's for kids. I got a better idea. Why don't we play the game of Building and Loan?"

"Sounds good to me. How do we play it?"

"It's real easy," she replied. "You just leave the building and leave me alone."

———⟫●⟪———

The United Fund volunteer called on the town's richest woman and asked for a contribution, saying, "I was honored to find your name on my list because you are rumored to be the most generous woman in town."

The woman wrote out a check and handed it to the man, saying, "There's a check for ten dollars. Now you can start denying the rumor."

DAVE CARPENTER...

"I'm also just rank and file, you'll have to ask the shop steward?"

A golfer had finished getting out of a sand trap and his ball lay about two feet from the hole. A lady, with his four-some, had her ball lying some 20 feet from the hole. She was about to putt when the first golfer said, "The traps on this course sure are a pain in the neck, aren't they?"

The woman, about to putt, said, "They sure are. And now would you kindly shut yours!"

————

A mother was telling her little boy about her life on the farm where she had grown up. "I had a swing made of an old automobile tire and swung from our old oak tree, and I rode a little pony and I used to slide down the haystack in the fall and ride our sleigh in the winter."

Her little boy heaved a great sigh and said, "I sure wish I had met you sooner."

Grandma was visiting her son and his family for the first time. Their little three-year old daughter was fascinated with her grandma, especially with her false teeth and wig. She watched with devoted attention as Grandma removed them at night.

"Do that once more, Grandma. That's fun."

And Grandma obliged the little girl by doing just that. "Now what do you want me to do?" Grandma asked.

"Now, please, Grandma, let me see you remove your ears."

———————

A little boy wrote his Grandmother: "Dear Grandma, I'm sorry that I forgot your birthday last week. It would certainly serve me right if you forgot mine next Monday."

———————

Sally was talking on the telephone about her roommate: "Betty's still in bed. She's got a terrible hangover this morning."

"Oh, was she at a wild party last night?"

"No! She came here on the late champagne flight from Los Angeles last night and the plane was stuck in a holding pattern over the airport for two hours."

———————

A postal clerk in Springfield, Illinois, tried to do a favor to a young guy when he sold him 100 special stamps with Canadian geese as the emblem. In a few hours the young man came back and said, "These stamps are not right for us, we're using them to go on a wedding invitation and my fiancee thinks this bird looks too much like a stork!"

One young lady to another: "It's the tiny things I like most about him — like, he owns a little mansion, a little yacht and a little racing stable. Plus he's President of the town's littlest bank."

———>●<———

We should act toward our government just as women act toward their husband, the man they love; a wife who loves her man will do anything for him except stop criticizing and trying to improve him.

———>●<———

Mamie responded to a question from her friend: "You ask what were the happiest days of my younger married life? School days, that was it! When the children got old enough to go."

———>●<———

Tom: "How is it that you never want to go skiing with me?" Sally: "Well, Tom, I will tell you why. It's a kind of a joie dementia that I prefer to enjoy in absentia."

———>●<———

At the Naval base, a young marine was enchanted by a pin worn by a young lady. The pin showed a cluster of naval signaling flags. She saw his admiring stare and said, "I see you're admiring my brooch. It was a present from my husband, and the flags mean 'I Love You'."

Knowing that the word "Love" was not in the Naval Signal Manual, the marine returned to his quarters and got out his manual. He discovered that the flag meant: "Permission to lay alongside."

A woman was being questioned by a licensed department inspector and was tickled when the inspector asked: "Have you ever been examined and found insane or feeble-minded...that is, by anyone other than your own kids?"

———⟫●⟪———

A minister was offering a sermon and the subject was heaven. He asked all those who desired to go to heaven to stand. All but one woman stood. Then the minister asked those who preferred going to hell to stand. Nobody stood. That puzzled the preacher, who looked down at the lone woman, sitting there and asked where she wanted to go. "Nowhere," she replied, "I like it just fine right here."

———⟫●⟪———

Helen Morgan was at a cocktail party, holding a rum and Coca-Cola, when the maid appeared with a tray of canapés. The maid was quite insistent on serving Helen who told her, "No thanks, once again, I belong to Hors D'oeuvres Anonymous."

———⟫●⟪———

In a Chicago newspaper, a classified advertisement appeared that read: Wanted; A job for a young woman. To hell with housework.

———⟫●⟪———

A high school English teacher met one of her students in the hall. The student asked: "Tell me, Ma'am, what's your judgment on the big game Saturday? You don't think we'll do too bad, do you?"

"I think you mean badly," she replied.

"What's the diff!" the boy replied. "You know what I mean."

"An L-Y can make quite a difference," she replied, pointing to a girl student with a good figure. "Take her, for example, it makes a lot of difference whether you look at her sternly or merely at her stern."

"I'll put in my 98¢ worth and then you put in you 2¢ worth."

The family was talking about their very self-centered maiden aunt. The mother, angry at the latest demands said, "What Sarah Jane needs is to lose someone she loves very much."

Grandma nodded and said, "A good point, my dear, but you can't cry at your own funeral."

———

The young girl was trying out various perfumes. Finally she told the clerk: "Can't you find a perfume for me that'll bring out the mink in a man without disturbing the wolf?"

Nurse to daddy waiting in the waiting room. "Sir, now you have a possible future president of the United States...if we ever have the judgment to elect a woman."

———➤●◄———

The wife of a business executive came to his office in late afternoon. They were to have dinner out that night. As they were going down in the elevator, it stopped and a slick, cute blonde got on. She poked the husband in the ribs and said, "Howdy, cutie pie."

Not a bit bothered, the wife said, with a smile, "Let me introduce myself. I'm Mrs. Pie."

———➤●◄———

The wife interrupted her knitting of a tiny garment to say to her husband: "Gosh, dear, I meant to tell you...it wasn't psychosomatic after all."

———➤●◄———

A guy is going down the street when he meets God. He asks God: "Why did you make women so beautiful?"

God replies: "So you'll love them."

Then he asks: "Why did you make women so soft?"

God replies: "So you'll love them."

Then the guy asks: "Why did you make women so dern stupid?"

God replies: "So they will love you."

———➤●◄———

An English teacher advised her class: "If you want to succeed in life, get a large vocabulary. Use a word ten times and it'll be yours." In the back of the room sat Becky who had a crush on Bob. She was heard repeating; "Bob, Bob, Bob, Bob, Bob, Bob, Bob, Bob, Bob, Bob!"

A young fellow was trying to impress his sweetheart: "Darling, tomorrow is Valentine's Day. That's the day for sweethearts, when two hearts melt into one. Isn't it amazing that this time last year, I didn't even know you?"

"It's delightful that we're together now," she said, nodding in agreement. Then she said: "Let's talk about my present."

A woman had just paid a $45.00 fine for a traffic violation. The woman who was clerk of the Court gave her a receipt. "What good is this receipt?" the woman complained.

"You should file it in a good place," the clerk replied. "Because when you get four of them, you get a bicycle."

A woman close to 90 was asked to what she attributed her long life. "I think," she replied, "it's because many a night I went to bed and slept when I should have stayed up and worried."

She told the guy he looked like a million, and she meant every penny of it!

———›●‹———

"Everything is relative," the 90-year-old lady told her grandchildren. "Now when I drop and break a mirror, I'm delighted because I know I'll have another 7 years of bad luck."

———›●‹———

The woman went to the physician about her ears. "What's the matter?" asked the doctor. "Are you having hearing trouble?"

"Nope," she replied. "That's not it. It's overhearing that bothers me."

———›●‹———

The doctor came into the prep room before the operation and said to elderly Mrs. Simpson: "Madam, I have to tell you that only about one in four survive this operation. Before we begin is there anything I can do for you?"

"Yes," replied the patient, "Hand me my shoes, stockings, and dress, please."

———›●‹———

A young guy with nothing to do heard about a high society party and decided to crash it. He did, had plenty to eat and drink and had a great time. As the guests were leaving, he got in line and when he came to the hostess said, "Thank you so much. It's been a superb party."

"Glad you enjoyed it," said the hostess. "Remind me to invite you next time."

———›●‹———

Did you hear about the guy who told the girl that his heart belonged to her? She didn't like it because the rest of him was going out with other girls.

One woman to another: "Oh, Fred and I have our arguments, but nothing that Blue Cross doesn't cover."

———>●<———

At a lecture, the speaker began to ask the audience questions. One of them began: "Is there anyone in the audience who would let her husband be slandered and say nothing?"

An old woman stood and the speaker yelled: "Do you mean to say you'd let your husband be slandered and say nothing?"

"Oh, I'm sure sorry, Mr. Speaker. I misunderstood you. I thought you said slaughtered."

———>●<———

The wealthy old woman was asked to what she attributed her long life. "I believe God has allowed me to reach this age because he wanted to test the patience of my relatives."

———>●<———

A guy drove into a gasoline station and asked for one gallon of gas. The woman attendant asked him: "What are you trying to do...wean it?"

———>●<———

Two teenagers were having a discussion about their parents. One said her parents never argued. The other said, "That's wonderful. Must be a superb marriage."

"It's not so much that, as that when Mom tells Dad to do something, he does it!"

———>●<———

In Southern Illinois a woman got on the train and handed the ticket to the conductor. He looked at it and said, "This ticket is no good, it's <u>from</u>, not <u>to</u>."

"What the dickens is the difference?" the woman exclaimed. "It's the same both ways in fare...isn't it?"

"It is, but I can't take this ticket," the conductor flatly stated.

"How'll it be if I ride backwards," the lady said. "Would that do the trick?"

The driver shrugged, accepted the ticket and that was that.

———⟫●⟪———

Two old friends were arguing about the forthcoming wedding of the 60-year-old with a young girl in her twenties. "The younger, 50-year-old guy said, "I don't believe in these Spring, Winter marriages. For certain winter will find in spring the loveliness of you. But what on earth is spring going to find in December?"

"Christmas," was the response.

———⟫●⟪———

When winter comes, many a man digs a path so his wife can go to work...thus proving that shovelry is not dead.

> John A Fenn
> West Palm Beach, Florida

———⟫●⟪———

Autoeroticism: Necking in a car.

———⟫●⟪———

Two young ladies were chatting over coffee. "Tell me, dear, how are things going with your new boyfriend?" one asked.

"Oh, I got rid of him, already," the other replied. "By the time we had our second date, I discovered a split personality and that I couldn't tolerate either one."

The woman was running for her state legislature and stopped off to talk to a farmer who was working in his garden.

"Here's my card," she said, "and I'd appreciate it if you'd vote for me."

"Vote for you," the farmer shouted, "Why I'd rather vote for the devil himself."

"Well, in case your friend decides not to run, I'd like you to vote for me," she replied.

———⟫●⟪———

The preacher in a small town was being transferred to a big city and he was torn between going and staying with the smaller community. He told his family that he would give the matter a lot of prayer.

A week later a friend asked the six-year-old daughter if her father had decided what to do.

"I'm not sure," was the reply. "He's still praying and Mom is packing."

———⟫●⟪———

"How do you like your new boss?" one secretary asked another during their lunch.

"He's all right, I suppose. But he's just too darned prejudiced."

"You mean over women's lib and black and white and all that?"

"Oh not. Not at all. It's just that he thinks there's only one way to spell a word."

———⟫●⟪———

A woman was attending a large dinner party and the pre-dinner drinks were being served. She discovered that only fruit juice and punch were to be had.

When the host announced that dinner was served, she picked up her coat and started to leave the room. "You aren't going are you?" the host asked her. "We're just about to begin dinner."

"I know," the woman said, "but I never eat on an empty stomach."

———⇒●⇐———

A woman and her husband checked into a hotel for the night. But they'd been driving for hours and the wife had to go. She asked the desk clerk if she could use the restroom. He gave her a key and directions. "We always keep our bathroom locked," he told the woman.

"Why, are you afraid someone will break in and clean it?" she replied.

———⇒●⇐———

Two women were riding in a bus seated next to each other. One said, "I'm from Aspen, Colorado and you?"

"I'm from Cincinnati, Ohio," the other replied.

"In Aspen, we put all our emphasis on breeding," said the woman.

"We do, too, in Cincinnati," the other replied, "but we try to see a movie on some nights."

———⇒●⇐———

Dear Johnny: I owe you a thousand apologies and I want to tell you that I love you very much. I hope you'll find it possible to forgive me. I've finally got my life back together again and I want you to be a part of it. Please call me soon as I very much want to see you again.

Mabel

P.S. And I do want to congratulate you on winning the lottery.

———⇒●⇐———

How do you handle a pest who just won't leave you alone? Well, here's the way one girl did it when the fellows persisted in asking for her phone number. She gave it to them but when they called her number, the reply was: "Pest Control Helpers."

It had been over a year since the widow Brown had lost her husband and now she admitted frankly to her friends that she was very lonely. She decided to attend her church's service for the first time since the death. The minister recognized her and said to the congregation, "Mrs. Brown is now in church for the first time since her husband's death. So we want to honor her by letting her select the next three hymns. Mrs. Brown?"

Mrs. Brown smiled and looked at three good-looking young men, saying: "I choose him and him and him."

"Hi – I'm the ghost of marriage past...here to pick up my alimony check."

Jimmy and Betty were on their first date and Jimmy began the conversation by saying, "I'm seeking a wife who likes to cook, clean house, sew clothes, keep the house clean and doesn't run around with her girls friends, or drink, or smoke."

Betty replied: "Tell you what, man, why don't you go to the cemetery and dig yourself up one?"

———>>●<<———

The cute, pretty girl had just broken up with her doctor boyfriend.

"Are you telling me," exclaimed her girlfriend, "that the bastard asked you to give back all those presents he gave you while you were going together?"

"Yep! Not only that, but he sent me a bill for 152 house calls!"

———>>●<<———

Definition of a shotgun wedding: A case of wife or death.

"Burt, don't jump, you're wearing my Rolex!"

The hill-billie farmer called the doctor and asked him to take a look at his son-in-law. "I shot him this morning and nicked his cheek."

"Shame on you!" the doctor yelled. "Shooting your son-in-law!"

"Well, Doc, he wasn't my son-in-law when I shot him!"

———>●<———

Two women were shopping at the supermarket and one said, "Sylvia, isn't that a new dress you're wearing?"

"Sure is. I bought it for my birthday. Hubby never recalls the date so he tells me to buy my own birthday present."

"It must drive you wild to have a husband who can't remember such intimate things as your birthday."

"Don't be silly! This is my fourth dress this year."

———>●<———

The toughest thing for most wives to get used to after marriage is being whistled for...not at.

———>●<———

An innocent old lady was drinking a martini for the first time in her life. She sipped it, then said, "This tastes just like the medicine my husband has been taking for years."

———>●<———

The businessman returned home from work to find the house in total disarray.

"What is going on here? It's a mess!" he told his wife. "How come?"

"Well, you're always asking me what I do all day and today I didn't do it."

Two women were playing golf, when a funeral procession went by. Her partner bowed her head and her friend said: "That's a mighty nice gesture on your part."

"It's the least I can do. After all, we were married for forty years."

———⇒⊃●⊂⇐———

Husband and wife were having another argument. "I'm willing to meet you half way," the wife said, "I'll admit I'm wrong if you'll admit I'm right."

———⇒⊃●⊂⇐———

Clever Mollie

A rich man had a hill girl for a maid. Her name was Mollie, and she was smart, but oh, so lazy! One day the rich man called a friend to come to dinner, and he ordered Mollie to make great preparations. She cooked 'em two chickens, one apiece, and the rich man bought a bottle of wine. Then he said, "If only we had finger sandwiches!"

Mollie'd not heard of such a thing, but she said nothing. The rich man went to fetch his friend home, and Mollie set out the plates, and poured the wine. She tasted the wine to see if it was good. She tasted it several times.

Then she tasted the chickens. She tasted them several times, too. Soon the wine was all gone, and the chickens were bones.

Here come the rich man, putting on airs, bringing his friend along. He set the friend in the parlor and said, "If only we had finger sandwiches!"

He'd just about figured that the wine was gone when Mollie knew she had to think fast. The rich man took out the carving knife to carve on the chickens, and Mollie ran to the parlor and said to the guest, "He's crazy. He's got the knife to cut off your hands and make finger sandwiches!"

Out came the rich man with the knife. The guest hollered out, and ran from the house. Mollie said, "While you was in the kitchen, your guest et one chicken and took the other to home. He drank all the wine, too!"

The rich man ran out with his knife, hollering, "Just leave one! Just leave one!"

The guest put his hands in his pockets and hollered out, and ran on, and never saw the rich man again. Mollie laughed, and laughed, and the rich man never knew! Clever Mollie!

> Richard and Judy Dockery Young
> *Ozark Tall Tales*
> Reprinted with permission of
> August House
> 1989

The twenty best years of a woman's life are between 39 and 40.

There's a woman down in our town who saves lots of money by doing plastic surgery...she destroyed all of her husband's credit cards!

"What would you like for your birthday?" the insurance salesman asked his wife.

"I'd like to have something that's hard to break," she replied.

"You refer to something like Tupperware?" he asked.

"No, not that," she replied. "I was thinking of something more in the line of a hundred dollar bill."

Albert Lyons was trying to get himself out of the dog-house with his wife.

"Tell me, dear," he asked, "What kind of present shall I buy for the one I love best?"

"Go get a big stogie and a six pack," she replied.

Waiting...
for the perfect man!

Two motorists met on a very narrow bridge and could not pass.

"I will never back up for a damned fool," yelled the guy in the Chevy.

"That's ok," said the woman driver as she shifted to reverse, "I'll do it."

BIBLIOGRAPHY

A High Toned Woman, Joyce Gibson Roach, *Hoein' the Short Rows.* 1987. University of North Texas Press.

An Eternal Truth, Phyllis M. Letellier, *A Stock Tank of Petunias on Poverty Flat.* 1998. Timber Trails Publishing Company.

Aunt Jean's Marshmallow Fudge Diet, Jean Kerr, *Please Don't Eat the Daisies.* 1957. Doubleday.

Buty, Josh Billings, *America's Phunniest Phellow.* 1986. Lincoln-Herndon Press.

Clever Mollie, Richard and Judy Dockery Young, *Ozark Tall Tales.* 1989. August House.

Confessions of a Wild Bore, John Updike, *Assorted Prose.* 1965. Alfred A. Knopf.

Contented, Dorothy L. Wampler, *Motherhood to Menopause.* 1971.

Damned If I Will, Dorothy L. Wampler, *Motherhood to Menopause.* 1971.

Dickson's Joke Treasury, Paul Dickson. 1992. John Wiley & Sons.

Excerpts From You Can Never Go Wrong By Lying, Patricia Marx. 1985. Houghton Mifflin Publishing

Fathers, Dorothy L. Wampler, *Motherhood to Menopause.* 1971.

Female Remarks, Josh Billings, *America's Phunniest Phellow.* 1986. Lincoln-Herndon Press.

Gene Perret's Funny Business: Speaker's Treasury of Business Humor For All Occasions, Gene and Linda Perret. 1990. Prentice Hall Direct.

Grammar Lesson, James York Glimm, *Flatlanders and Ridgerunners: Folktales From the Mountains of Northern Pennsylvania.* 1983 University of Pittsburg Press

Greeting Exchange, Dorothy L Wampler, *Motherhood to Menopause.* 1971.

Home Management, Dorothy L Wampler, *Motherhood to Menopause.* 1971.

How a Lady Stopped a Train, James York Glimm, *Flatlanders and Ridgerunners: Folktales From the Mountains of Northern Pennsylvania.* 1983. University of Pittsburg Press.

How to Figure a Woman, Dorothy L. Wampler, *Motherhood to Menopause.* 1971.

How to Lose Friends, Billie D. Tressler, *How to Lose Friends and Alienate People.* 1937. Stackpole Books.

Man, Samuel Hoffenstein, *Year In, You're Out.* 1930. Liverlight Publishing.

Missing Outhouse, James Yok Glimm, *Flatlanders and Ridgerunners: Folktales From the Mountains of Northern Pennsylvania.* 1983. University of Pittsburg Press.

Motherhood Is Fine — If It Weren't For Kids, Phyllis M. Letellier, *A Stock Tank of Petunias on Poverty Flat.* 1998. Timber Trails Publishing Company.

On Columbia Discoverin' Woman, Marietta Holley, *Samantha on the Woman Question.* 1913.

On Hot Flashes, Dorothy L. Wampler, *Motherhood to Menopause.* 1971.

Proposition No. II, Dorothy L. Wampler, *Motherhood to Menopause.* 1971.

She Was Only a . . ., Quoted from *The Pelican.* 1960. University of California Press.

So Why Invest in a Man at All? Stephanie Brush, *Men: An Owner's Manual.* 1984. Simon & Schuster.

The Ovum, Samuel Hoffenstein, *Year In, You're Out.* 1930. Liverlight Publishing Company.

The Smart Husband and the Smarter Wife, M. Jagendorg, *New England Bean Pot.* 1948. VanGuard Press.

Three and a Half Husbands, Dorothy Fuldheim. 1976. John Carroll University, Cleveland.

Wages, Dorothy L. Wampler, *Motherhood to Menopause.* 1971.

Weekends, Barbara Holland, *Endangered Pleasures.* 1995. Little, Brown and Company.

CARTOONISTS:

Bucella, Martin — Cheektowaga, NY

Carpenter, Dave — Emmetsburg, IA

Corbett, Jack — Salem, OR

Estes, James — Amarillo, TX

Gaspirtz, Oliver — Brooklyn, NY

Hawkins, Johnny — Sherwood, MI

Linkert, Lo — Mission City, Canada

Masters Agency — Hollister, CA

Piro, Stephanie — Farmington, NH

Pletcher, E. L. — Slidell, LA

Rosandich, Dan — Chassell, MI

Schwadron, Harley — Ann Arbor, MI

Toos, Andrew — Newtown, CT

Also Available from Lincoln-Herndon Press: